DISCOVER A PROUD HERITAGE THROUGH ITS ANTIQUES

William Penn's liberal government attracted the leading artisans of Europe, setting the background for the explosion of art and culture in colonial Pennsylvania. The town of Philadelphia became the center of early American furniture production, responsible for the development of the beautiful American Windsor chair, the Philadelphia Chippendale cabinet, the first use of red leather as an upholstery material.

The English aristocrats who settled in Virginia combined an appreciation of the beautiful with a firm belief in hard work. They built a powerful colony with the sweat of their brows, while at the same time introducing the fine Jacobean style to the New World.

America wrought a remarkable change on the descendants of the hell-fire Puritan settlers, greatly affecting the items they lived with. For example, silverware, considered hateful and unholy by the original Massachusetts Pilgrims, reached the apex of fine design with the work of Paul Revere, a Boston craftsman.

Antiques are tangible survivors of times long gone. They reflect the thoughts, visions, tastes and physical surroundings of our forefathers. NEW GEOGRAPHY OF AMERICAN ANTIQUES can help you understand their origin and bring history into your home.

NEW GEOGRAPHY
of
AMERICAN ANTIQUES

Carl W. Drepperd

and

Lurelle Van Arsdale Guild

AWARD BOOKS • TANDEM BOOKS
NEW YORK LONDON

First printing, 1967

Copyright, 1927, by Doublday & Company, Inc.
Copyright, 1948, by Carl W. Drepperd and
Lurelle Van Arsdale Guild

Published by
Universal Publishing and Distributing Corporation
235 East 45th Street, New York, N. Y. 10017

Manufactured in the United States of America

CONTENTS

Chapter I

INTRODUCTION

THE first thing we shall do in this *New Geography of American Antiques* is consider the people who settled the original colonies. The things they brought with them from their homelands and the things they made for themselves or had made for them when here were our first antiques. The type of life that climate, isolation, and new opportunity forced the colonists to lead, the character they developed under these pressures, their religious and political affiliations, the degree of poverty or wealth they achieved, and the status in life which was their reward are all reflected in objects collected and designated today as American antiques.

Europe, during the century and a half of heaviest colonial migration to our American continent, 1601-1751, was in constant political and religious turmoil. The reigning houses of France, England, and Spain were not only at war with each other but frequently were unstable within themselves. After the Netherlands had achieved its freedom from Spain, the unholy word "republic" was heard in Europe. The Dutch Nation, beyond any shadow of a doubt, was the most liberal and tolerant in continental Europe. Through the exercise of these two qualities of character it became a great trading nation and brought to its ports the arts and the crafts of the Far East, paving the way, by Chinese influence, for the development, successively, of the so-called William and

Mary, Queen Anne, and Georgian styles of furniture. This same style influence filtered into France and became Louis XV. It was impressed upon England by virtue of the fact that England's internal strife had resulted in the execution of one Stuart king, an era of democracy under Cromwell which turned out to be the very worst kind of autocracy, the Restoration of the Stuart line, and the ultimate deposition of another Stuart king, at which point England invited William of Orange to the throne. William and Mary, dying without issue, were followed by another Stuart Restoration in the person of Queen Anne. She died without issue, and England again had to go out and hunt a ruler. They selected a petty German princeling who reigned over England as George I, the first of the House of Hanover which still—in theory, at least—rules England.

France, in the seventeenth century, had granted a measure of religious freedom to the Reformed or Protestant people. This was under the Edict of Nantes which Louis XIV revoked at the insistence of Cardinal Richelieu. The warrior cardinal captured Rochelle and broke the back of the Protestant movement in France. The Protestants fled to Flanders, Switzerland, Alsace-Lorraine, various German states, and the Netherlands. From there they had eyes on but one spot, America. Many of them managed to get to America and, once here, laid at the feet of their savior land everything they had in the way of mental equipment, knowledge, and craftsmanship.

When the Netherlands were under the heel of Spain, many Protestants were forced to flee or go into hiding. Some Dutch Protestants were followers of Menno Simons, a onetime Catholic priest. They emigrated to Russia, Poland, Switzerland, and the Palatine States. When they heard of a better land—America—and that

William Penn was offering religious freedom to all who came to his colony, they emigrated by shiploads to Pennsylvania. It has been thought that they carried with them only knowledge of how to till the soil. We now know, however, that they carried with them knowledge of how to snail a gun barrel and make the gun a rifle. They established a production of rifles in quantities which, in the hands of our Revolutionary Army, were a great contributing factor in the winning that war. In addition, Mennonites brought knowledge of fine clock-making and fine cabinetmaking.

In England all dissenters from the Established Church were subject to persecution. They, too, wanted to escape. By 1620 their escape route was established and so was the colony of Northern Virginia or Massachusetts Bay.

Spain, impotent within, was impotent also as a colonizing agent. Her whole philosophy was one of stripping any American possession of its gold, silver, and precious stones, and of killing all native American Indians who did not subject themselves to mass baptism.

The colonization movement in Virginia was not fully consolidated until the murder of King Charles I put the Puritans in power in England. Then it was the turn of the Royalists to find an escape route. They went to Virginia. The gentlemen who settled there, if they did not forget their free-and-easy life in Mother England, at least did not scorn to work with their own hands in order to help build a powerful colony. By 1770 this Royalist colony was working hand in hand with the Pilgrim colony of Massachusetts Bay to achieve an independence that would be common to both.

We know considerably more today than we knew twenty years ago about the homes of the first settlers from European lands who established themselves on these shores of ours. In the past two decades we have learned how to do research work and how to read social history from heretofore unconsidered documents. We now know that the first homes of all settlers were make-shifts—lean-tos, caves, or wigwams. We know these were set up until better homes could be built within the pattern to which the settler had been accustomed in his own state, style, and nation. We know that many substitutes had to be used for bricks, mortar, and other building materials. But we also know that within a few years traditional styles of construction were under way, and that the early American home was a reflection of either Elizabethan, Carolean, Dutch, Swedish, or French houses, large or small, imposing or humble.

We know also what was in these houses. As the settlers, inhabiting their second or their third domicile, died, they left wills and testaments in which articles of furniture are mentioned. Quite frequently the value of household goods is given in inventories. It is sensible to assume that a resident of Virginia, dying in 1670, and bequeathing four sets of fire irons and fire tools to four different beneficiaries, lived in a house having at least four fireplaces. That is simply putting two and two together. It is axiomatic that we use such techniques rather than hit-and-miss or guess techniques in reconstructing the early American scene as it was.

The research of Dr. Shurleff, one of the first consultants for the Williamsburg Restoration, exploded for all time the myth of the log cabin as the basic early American home. The log cabin was a mighty scarce article except in the New Sweden that is now Pennsylvania. There it was not a log cabin, but a log house, often of pretentious style and quality. This log construction of the Swedes also became the pattern that was followed on the frontiers and was the prototype of every blockhouse built from Lancaster, Pennsylvania, westward to Vincennes, Kaskaskia, and Fort Dearborn.

Elizabethan furniture, in the form of massive oak chests, tables, court cupboards, and press cupboards, was in Virginia and in New England during the so-called Pilgrim century. Perhaps some of it was in Maryland. The heavy chests and cabinet furniture of Dalecarlia and Skane, and comparable furniture from the Netherlands, were in what is now Pennsylvania long before 1680. The same kind of furniture that was in the homes of the mijnheers of Amsterdam and Rotterdam was also in the homes of the burghers of New Amsterdam, Yonkers, and Albany.

Whether this first furniture was made in Sweden, the Netherlands, and England, or whether it was made on these shores, is an arbitral point or a moot question. It really doesn't matter. Certainly some of it came over with the colonists and certainly some of it was brought over in the trade ships which kept up a constant line of communication between the various colonizing countries and companies and their colonies. The contents of several of the Swedish supply ships were tabulated and rested for some hundreds of years in the archives of Sweden. Now we know what was on board those ships, down to tips for flagpoles and woolen socks.

After the original colonization had been made, one of three things happened. The worst, of course, was the eradication of the colony—complete destruction by the death of the colonists and the burning of their culture by hostile native American Indians. Or the colony remained static and did not grow. Or the colony thrived. Most of the colonies thrived. Some thrived to such an extent that the population doubled every ten years. Twice the number of houses and double the amount of furniture were needed. That, in turn, meant importation of men who knew how to build the new homes and of men who could make the things necessary to furnish them. Many shiploads of people, destined for a thriving colony, carried silversmiths, pewterers, arkwrights, turners, joiners, and even artists. In scanning the lists of those who arrived we are sometimes amazed to discover that French cabinetmakers, decorators, and artisans settled in New England rather than in the French colony of New Rochelle in the province of New York. Appolos Revoire, or Paul Revere the first, chose to settle in Boston. Some Dutch cabinetmakers settled in Philadelphia rather than in New York. Many English cabinetmakers emigrated to New York, Philadelphia, Boston, and Charleston. There was a publicity campaign of no mean proportion current in the late seventeenth and early eighteenth centuries. William Penn was ready to promise almost anything to anybody if he would come to Pennsylvania to settle. Philadelphia became the cultural capital of the colonies within fifty years of its official founding and within one hundred years of its original settlement by the Swedes.

Even though we find no record of a journeyman cabinetmaker coming over on the *Mayflower* on its first or second trip, we do know that John Alden is credited with experience as a joiner, and that arkwrights, or ship carpenters, came over as early as 1623. These, undoubtedly, did a kind of cabinetmaking or "joining." This should not be surprising. There were very few cabinetmakers, as such, working in England at the same time. The arkwrights, the shipwrights, the joiners, and the turners were making most of the furniture for the English people.

When the Pilgrims left England for Massachusetts Bay, and when chivalry left England for Virginia, Elizabethan styles still persisted in the cottages and the homes of the British yeomen and artisans. The Jacobean style was the furniture of the manor houses and the palace.

The gentlemen adventurers who first came to Virginia did not care much about the sacrifices they had to make in order to recoup their fortunes. Their only thought was to get back to England and live in the manner to which they had formerly been accustomed. The later comers to Virginia were not fortune hunters, but exiles, determined to re-establish their pattern of life in a new land. Just how thoroughly Virginians carried on the feud with Cromwell and his cohorts can be gathered from the fact that their name of the object called a chamber pot in New England was "Oliver's Skull."

No matter how much difficulty the Swedes and the Dutch had along the South River, now called the Delaware River, things began to jell rapidly after Penn controlled the colony. Pennsylvania was prosperous from the very beginning. The Swedes and the Dutch who were on the spot were just as happy under the liberal government of William Penn—if not more so—as they had ever been under their own several governments. Penn's first settlers were not poor Quakers but well-to-do Quakers. Because Penn had rich lands to bestow upon poor immigrants, the poor immigrants did not remain poor very long. Thousands who came to Penn's colony before 1700 by 1710 were considered well-to-do, if not rich, people. Many of the Swiss immigrants to Pennsylvania after 1710 arrived with considerable funds obtained from the sale of their properties in Switzerland.

Historically we can trace the development of much furniture from a box, or coffer, used as a container for goods, and at times as a table or a seat. We can trace this movement quite readily in New England in what has been called Pilgrim furniture. We cannot properly appraise the term "Pilgrim" if we think it is to be applied only to a class of people. The term "Pilgrim" must be applied to all classes of people who were religiously or politically inclined in the same general direction. There were dissenters of great wealth and there were dissenters who were workmen on the estates of the wealthy dissenters. There were merchants, lawyers, ministers, teachers, yeomen, and yokels in the ranks of the dissenters. Many of these became Pilgrims—people ready to establish a new life in a new and wild country in order to enjoy living a religion which they fervently believed was the only pathway to heaven.

It is wrong, however, to think that New England began with Plymouth Rock. No less than forty recorded voyages preceded the Pilgrims to New England, and no less than fifty explorers had died in New England before the Puritans arrived. A colony of one hundred and twenty men had spent a year in New England a dozen years before the *Mayflower* arrived. This was the Popham Colony on the Kennebec River, planted by the Virginia Company. They traded in furs, cedar, and sassafras woods.

Permission was granted by Sir Walter Raleigh for further expeditions to "Northern Virginia," as New England was then known. Bristol merchants fitted out the *Speedwell* and the *Discoverer*, which left on a trading expedition in 1603. They reported codfish very plentiful at Casco Bay and, finally, cast anchor in Massachusetts Bay where they traded with the Indians, successfully cultivated small patches of ground, lived on the land, and went home with valuable and salable cargoes. English merchants were well aware of the possibilities of Northern Virginia. So were all of the crews that manned the trading ships. The Pilgrims and the Puritans did not come to found the colony of Massachusetts Bay by accident.

They came by design, knowing that unrivaled opportunities for making a good living and even for getting rich were united to religious freedom.

It has been said time after time by able analysts that we do wrong to ourselves and to the pioneers who settled this country when we pity them. In spite of what we read about their hardships, it was not always hardships, in relation to the general standard of living that obtained. If we read rightly between the lines, we can also read that with their hardships they also had one thumping good time. Hard cider and roast wild fowl for breakfast aren't exactly exemplary of a starvation diet!

Certainly the first furniture, other than the few sticks that came over with the *Mayflower* and succeeding vessels, was limited in scope and quality to a simple chest, an eating board, and a form or bench. We do not know precisely what kind of beds the colonists of New England enjoyed within the first ten years of their arrival. But it is likely that they had simple, cotlike structures or the single-post bed which, fitted into a corner of the room, had two of its sides supported against the wall and a post on the exposed corner to keep the bed level. Chairs were exceptionally scarce and important pieces. Old wills and inventories reveal that possession of two or three chairs was opulence. The rest of the seating was on the forms or benches that were common to all homes.

The first New England chests were built along the lines of the traditional English house chest of the fifteenth and sixteenth centuries. The sides of such chests were the only parts touching the floor. The body of the chest was kept off the floor, supported by side members which eventually became legs. These chests were almost always made of oak and quite frequently were paneled after the manner of Elizabethan house partition walls. They were solidly constructed, often having hand-wrought hinges and hand-wrought locks. Joints of stiles and rails were mortised and tenoned and held firm and secure by driving square pegs through round holes. Certain of these English chests were undoubtedly brought to New England, but within a few years after the colony was founded and the good town of Boston established, chest-making became the indoor occupation of the housewright, the joiner, and the arkwright.

When chest production began in New England, thinking about how to improve the chest also began. The first step was to put a drawer at the bottom of the chest, making the chest cavity smaller and providing access to at least a part of the piece without lifting the lid. Obviously the first thought after the one-drawer chest was made was "why not a two-drawer chest"? Then it became a three-drawer chest. And then the final flash of genius! No matter how small the chest cavity, one always had to lift the lid to get at it. That meant taking off the lid whatever was resting on it. So a fourth drawer was put in it and the chest lid was pegged or nailed down. That's how the chest of drawers was developed. But that isn't all that happened. The chest with one, two, three, or four drawers, and particularly the chests with two drawers, were embellished with carved and applied ornamentation—some of them ornate enough to cause the uninitiated to wonder whether the Pilgrims and the Puritans became very worldly overnight. The chests made at Hadley, Massachusetts, and at Hartford and other points in the Connecticut Valley, show very engaging tulip and sunflower motif carvings. A delightful three-drawer chest without a cavity under the lid was made in New England at Taunton, Massachusetts, by a group of Huguenot refugees. These chests, which date from around the year 1700, are decorated over the entire front with open scrolls, tulips, and facing bird designs. Two-drawer chests with painted fronts in imitation of the carving on older chests were apparently in general use in the last half of the seventeenth century, especially in the home of the less fortunate souls who were not making fortunes in trade but who were gaining a competence in farming and in the work of the various crafts.

No consideration of the chest proper is complete unless it includes the smaller chests, called desk boxes and Bible boxes. The desk box had quite an evolution of its own in New England. First examples are small chests with either flat or sloping lids, always having a lock and key. The Bible box, usually looking like a desk box, did not have a lock and key. The Bible, greatly respected, and considered the chief treasure of every household lucky enough to own one, was never locked up. The hottest fires of hell were kept burning for those whose sin was Bible stealing. Hence there was no fear of losing a Bible by theft. Every member of the family had access to the Bible—no lock, no key, on the Bible box. On the other hand, precious deeds and correspondence, not to mention bills of sale, inventories, and hard money, were kept under lock and key in the desk box. As trade increased, the desk box had a drawer added to it. Then it was further enlarged and had legs added. Then it was still further enlarged and placed in a frame of table-like dimensions. That is how the desk on frame developed in New England.

When we view New England as a colony we are apt to overlook the fact that it was actually a collection of colonies. The colonization of New England, after the first colony was planted, is but a repetition of what happened in England to cause the Pilgrims and the Puritans to cross the ocean and settle here. When they arrived, the dissenters managed to achieve considerable dissension among themselves. Rhode Island and Connecticut became separate colonial efforts, breaking away from the original Massachusetts Bay group. Boston soon became a busy trading port. The part of the colony within fifty miles of Boston had fairly regular communication with old England. Rhode Island, the Providence plantations, and the Connecticut Valley settlements did not immediately enjoy such communication. They continued in the old English tradition of chest-making, contributing their own innovations and developing their own style of decoration.

It is fairly certain that the desk box on frame with the sloping falling front, supported by two pull-out slides, was not wholly a New England development. It was an adaptation from furniture ideas that had slipped over the border from the Dutch colony of New York or directly from old England.

It is also likely that the chest on frame, now among the rarest of all chest types, was a New England adaptation of the court cupboard. The best examples look like simple court cupboards yet access to the interior is by one or more drawers and a lift-up top. Of surviving examples, some are plain, some painted, and some scratch carved. The fronts of the drawers have molding applied to simulate paneling. The legs are usually turned—a characteristic of simpler Jacobean furniture styling.

The furniture now called William and Mary, while Dutch in origin and developed by the Dutch from Chinese styles, may have entered New England by way of New York before old England accepted the style on the ascension of William and Mary to the throne of England. It would be entirely logical to assume this if more early William-and-Mary-style furniture was found in Connecticut and western Massachusetts than in and around Boston. According to most early observers, including Dr. Charles Woolsey Lyon, this seems to have been the case. Thus we have evidence of Hudson Valley influence in western New England. This same William-and-Mary-style furniture was in what is now Pennsylvania before William Penn arrived. The Dutch, in any colonizing effort, had it before William and Mary were sovereigns of England.

The first examples of Queen Anne furniture are an adaptation of William and Mary with the substitution of cabriole legs for deeply turned cup-and-ball and trumpet-turned legs. Variants of the Queen Anne style and the various stages of that style, now called Georgian and Chippendale, were made in New England, New York, New Jersey, Maryland, and Pennsylvania by many cabinetmakers. But the style did not originate with them. They followed the prevailing styles of England, in order to fill the demands of their customers.

The furniture really peculiar to New England includes the pine settle and the turned-stick chairs that are today generally characterized as the Brewster and Carver chairs. New England made that other and even more comfortable stick chair known as the Windsor, but the chair known as Windsor did not originate in New England—it is part of the Pennsylvania story. Wainscot chairs were made in New England, New York, and Pennsylvania. The logical successors of these chairs—banister-back and slat-back chairs—were made in most of the colonies in considerable quantities.

The chair became a factor in colonial life after 1660. Between that year and the year 1700 the roster of chairs made and used in the colonies includes the wainscot, Carver, Brewster, slat-back, banister-back, Carolean, splat-back, heart-back, Cromwellian, and Flemish. All of these are illustrated.

The printed word permits us to describe the various shapes and forms of cabinetwork we call furniture. But no word and no pictures can reproduce the feel and the texture of old woods. This is a quality of sensitiveness you can acquire only through years of experience of the sort commonly called practical, but which includes a quality of mind closely allied to affection. Which is to say you must love old things before you can appreciate them. If you love them only for their texture and feel, your love is shallow. If you love them only for what they are, your love still lacks depth. The objects dealt with in this *New Geography of American Antiques* have both physical and spiritual qualities. They are the visible, concrete extensions of a state of mind that was freedom in action. American antiques made before 1770 reflect a kind of freedom destined for fulfillment. American antiques after 1785 reflect that fulfillment.

We must study the great spiritual, social, and political forces which contributed to the creation of a nation before we can understand the significance of the changes that take place in the furniture of that nation. Every country, in some degree, reflects in the furniture made by and for its people the sentiments, aspirations, and intellectual qualities of the people.

We can, to an amazing degree, trace the strength and the weaknesses of governments, the vitiating qualities of prohibitive measures established by despots, and by wars and internal strife, by looking at the unconscious reflection of these things in the furniture of the people. The history of furniture styles is in itself an almost comprehensive history of the nations which produced the styles.

When we review the American scene from Plymouth

Rock and Jamestown through to the middle of the nineteenth century, we review in effect a vast number of people who, coming to a new land, experienced new stimuli which, in turn, produced different effects because of a definite change in their state of mind.

The melting pot of colonial America was the province of Pennsylvania. It began as a melting pot forty years before William Penn was given title to the land by the English sovereign. By 1640 the Swedes and a few Finns were in what is now Pennsylvania. At that time they established a new idea in home construction—the all-log house. Swedes in Pennsylvania also built brick houses and stone houses, and in so doing established a style of architecture admirably adapted to the climate of the country, and which persisted as a style until at least the mid-1850s. That it has been wrongly called Pennsylvania-German, or attributed to Swiss influence is, perhaps, a pardonable if not a reasonable error.

There was something of a battle fought between the Dutch and the Swedes for supremacy in the land along the South River. The Dutch called it the South River to differentiate it from the North River, now known as the Hudson River. The Dutch in New York, time after time, after Penn obtained title to the land, referred to their brethren in Pennsylvania as the Pennsylvania Dutch. The original Pennsylvania Dutch, to the Dutch of New York, were brothers of the New Jersey Dutch—Dutchmen living out of the original colony of New Amsterdam.

In this volume we shall attempt to trace the movements of racial, radical, and benign influences, and to show how they were merged and fused, in some cases completely obliterating the type of thinking that characterized Englishmen and Europeans at home and which, in America, developed a state of mind that was essentially free and consequently capable of great inductive reasoning and enjoying greater creative capacity.

One of our practical philosophers in 1810, looking at the hundred years of history that stood behind him and the hundred years which he chose to see stretching ahead for his new world, said, in effect: "We are not by nature better endowed with brains or knowledge than any other people on earth. But the way we live and the ease by which we achieve a living give us time for mental activity that can contemplate the vast resources of hitherto undreamed-of possibilities. It is because we have a shortage of laboring hands that we have taken to the machines as a means of producing things." In this our philosopher but echoed another unquestionably American product, Benjamin Franklin, who rolled up the whole thing into one neat phrase when he said, "Do not squander time, for time is the stuff life's made of."

Many historians have felt that the development of the thirteen colonies along the Atlantic seaboard, within the pattern of an English political and economic system, should have developed also an unbreakable bond between the colonies and the mother country. But three thousand miles of ocean separated the mother country and the colonies. Independence of a sort was literally forced on colonists by circumstances, conditions, and events. They simply had to exercise ingenuity in order to prosper. In the very earliest days they had to exercise ingenuity or die. This developed two kinds of thinking on the same subject three thousand miles apart. In old England they wanted to retain the pattern in which they had been cast. In the colonies they began to doubt the bona fides of the mold and sought ways and means by which it could be improved.

This thinking went on in all of the colonies and created a political unification without the people themselves being consciously aware of it. That unification has left its effect upon the furniture which is today collected by thousands of people under the generic term "American antiques."

Many experts in the field of art have complained of our laxity and our tardiness in producing a really great period of furniture. These experts have failed, somehow, to grasp the fact that in principle, at least, the greatest piece of furniture ever created by the people in this land was not made of wood. It was written on paper and is commonly known as the Constitution. It is because of the kind of thinking that developed the Constitution that we had men who, as cabinetmakers, could do precisely the same thing with the styles of other nations, and make them just different enough to be masterpieces within their own right.

We may speak glibly or we may speak in hushed admiration of cabinetmakers such as Savery, Randolph, Goddard, Gostelow, and Duncan Phyfe. But these men were not demigods. They are not to be classed with Chippendale, Hepplewhite, Sheraton, or the brothers Adam.

Perhaps another century or two will be required to fuse this nation of ours and its various people into one homogeneous whole. To this generation falls a part of that task. And a part of that task is appreciation of the background that has produced the American things we today collect as antiques.

EARLY VIRGINIA COURT CUPBOARD WITH APPLIED CORBELS

Chapter II

VIRGINIA

THE Virginia Company established the first permanent white settlement within the thirteen colonies. It was a trading company organized to make money for its stockholders. It is doubtful whether any furniture brought over for the convenience of the settlers at Jamestown survived that ill-starred and ill-fated spot. But by 1633 what is now Williamsburg was founded and the planting of settlements in Virginia, along its many inland waterways, went on apace.

The furniture brought over by these settlers and the furniture made for them was largely in the Elizabethan tradition. This is to say that in Virginia the court and the press cupboard and the massive Tudor bed were the chief articles of early seventeenth century furniture. It is probable that considerably more of this Elizabethan furniture—constructed largely of oak—was used in Virginia than in the colony of Massachusetts Bay or Massachusetts.

The colonization of Virginia was vastly improved by the influx of hundreds and thousands of Cavaliers and Royalists. In many cases these were forced to abandon their residences in England after the murder of King Charles I by Cromwell and his followers and the establishment of the dictatorship that was known in England as the Commonwealth. These seventeenth-century settlers brought to Virginia the finer furniture of the court

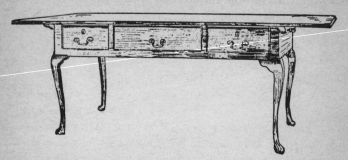

TYPICAL VIRGINIA QUEEN ANNE WALNUT LIBRARY TABLE

OAK PRESS

of King Charles—the furniture now called Jacobean. The Jacobean influence in England after 1603 was largely restricted to the court and the homes of the nobles and gentry. The Elizabethan style, in its various forms, became the furniture of the middle class and of the people in general.

It is quite natural that the men who settled Virginia brought with them Jacobean furniture and furnished their homes with what they had brought over, or reasonable facsimiles thereof. In Virginia the Royalist settlers succeeded in reproducing the typical English mansion, or manor house, of the period. This was a large square or rectangular central edifice with low wings at either or both sides. These houses were largely of masonry construction. Even at Jamestown some of the first efforts to build structures involved the use of masonry built of bricks. It is recorded that the first entire brick house in Virginia was built in 1638. This was twenty-two years before Gunnar Rambo, the Swede, built what is believed to be the first brick house in the Swedish settlement that became Philadelphia.

A quotation from a narrative concerning the founding of Henrico, Virginia, gives us some information concerning the exteriors of the houses: "And to answer the first objection for holesome lodging, here they have built competent and decent houses, the first stories all of brick, etc." We see here an expression of the Jacobean tradition in architecture that was not duplicated anywhere in New England or in the middle Atlantic colonies. From descriptions obtained from wills, letters, and similar sources we may compound a general idea of the interiors of such homes. Low, long rooms, with chamfered center and cross beams, were characteristic. In many rooms rectangular paneling, set into rails and stiles, was used. In other instances the walls were covered with wainscot sheathing. Windows were small and few in number, and were either fitted with small leaded panes or provided with wooden shutters.

Early Virginia furniture, in almost every known instance, retained rectangular forms and followed with little variation the elements of the Elizabethan or Tudor style. We know that nearly all of this early furniture in Virginia was made of oak, and we could go on indefinitely quoting proof of this from old wills and inventories. But, unfortunately, extant examples are rarities today. We may attribute this to two facts. In the first place, the Virginia settlers, being men of means and not without position in the mother country, were able to import furniture and, as the colony grew, established a trade to bring to their ports fine furniture made abroad. When a new fad appeared from overseas, furniture in use here was thrown into discard and replaced with imports. As a rule the discarded furniture found its way to slave houses and, in time, was destroyed by hard use.

Because the settlers were not forced by circumstances to make their own new furniture, but imported whatever the connoisseurs of the mother country were sponsoring at the moment, very little early Virginia furniture was saved. Today we must study the furniture of early Virginians from the few extant pieces and from written records of the times.

So far as we know, the range of pieces in this country was similar to that in England, and consisted in a large part of chests, tables, a few chairs, many forms, joined stools, cupboards, and state beds. The oak period of Virginia lasted perhaps for less than fifty years. It was followed by Jacobean-style furniture, some made on the spot, of Virginia walnut and other native woods.

In the field of early oak the chairs were of the wainscot variety, formal and dignified in appearance. These were

HERRINGBONE HIGHBOY WITH CROSS STRETCHER

armchairs the front legs of which were carried up to form posts for the arms. The seats were almost all of wood construction and, when originally used, were supplied with loose cushions covered with leather or fancy fabrics. Side chairs were generally joined stools looking very much like small tables, and sometimes fitted with drawers. The bench known as the "form" was simply an elongated joined stool and was used generally for seating in the dining hall, one at each side of the long table, at the head and foot of which stood wainscot chairs. Early Virginia inventories sometimes mention a livery cupboard. This is an exceptionally rare type of cupboard in the American scene.

Oak buffets, press cupboards, and court cupboards of very ornate quality adorned the Virginia home until the last few decades of the seventeenth century. By that time the trend was toward either modifications of the Jacobean styles or to the more modern styles enjoyed by Virginia's fellow colonies New York and Pennsylvania— the furniture known as William and Mary.

It should be noted that the so-called Jacobean style is an English adaptation of Dutch and Flemish styles which, in the Netherlands and Flanders, were refined into what is now called William and Mary. The twist-turned and twist-carved legs on certain Jacobean tables and chairs are found also on early William and Mary furniture.

Early William and Mary furniture in Virginia includes examples that apparently were made nowhere else in the colonies. In this category falls the gated-front fold-over-top table and the gated-front slope-fall desk. These tables are variants of the gate-leg table which, in its Jacobean form, made in Virginia of Virginia walnut, displays baluster turnings quite different from those found in New York, Massachusetts, or Pennsylvania.

PANELED OAK SETTEE

HEPPLEWHITE PAINTED FIVE-BACK SETTEE

HEPPLEWHITE UPHOLSTERED SOFA

As early as 1725 Virginia was importing furniture from Boston, New York, and Philadelphia, and employing some cabinetmakers of its own to produce the considerable volume of fine furniture required by the ever-increasing number of important plantations. Almost every Virginia country home was in the tradition of Westover, the famous manor built by the Byrds in the early 1730s. Very few Virginia homes duplicated that great mansion, but the philosophy was that of establishing a main house that was the headquarters for vast acreages of productive soil. Virginia, having the greatest population of any of the colonies at the time of the Revolution, did not have populated cities and towns in numbers comparable to other colonies. Virginia was well settled, throughout its Tidewater section. It was a veritable garden of great estates, county seats, and occasional small towns.

Virginia furniture from 1680 onward shows, successively, the finest trends in William and Mary, Queen Anne, Georgian, Chippendale, Adam, Hepplewhite, Directoire, and Sheraton styles. Too little has been written about the antiques of Virginia and too little attention has been given to the antiques of this great region mainly because the first important efforts at comments on early American furniture were based on New England examples. It is, however, well known that during the war period, 1861-65, many Virginia homes were looted of what can be today designated as their finest antiques.

Many families were also impoverished by that war and lost so many sons in the conflict that the families eventually died out. Furniture from hundreds of early Virginia homes found its way to the antique shops of Richmond and Baltimore, from whence it was sold to other dealers who often designated it as of Maryland, Pennsylvania, or even New York or New England origin. One of the finest antique shops in America today main-

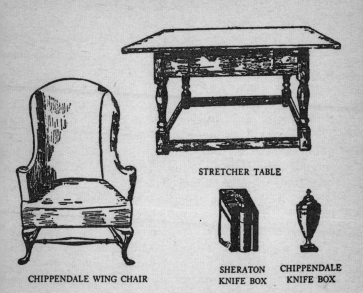

STRETCHER TABLE

CHIPPENDALE WING CHAIR

SHERATON
KNIFE BOX

CHIPPENDALE
KNIFE BOX

HEPPLEWHITE DINING TABLE

tains a broad avenue of communication with Virginia, and a large proportion of its finest stock comes out of the state traditionally known as the Old Dominion. It can be said without any shadow of doubt or without fear of contradiction that Virginia reflected the highest styles of the Elizabethan and the Carolean periods in America, and that its furniture of all other periods was as good as, if not better than, that of Boston or New York. After 1750 Philadelphia's exclusively made Georgian-style furniture became the favorite with the wealthy people of Virginia. The shipmasters of Philadelphia carried on a brisk trade with the Virginia Tidewater ports, and directly with many Tidewater plantations, most of which had their own docks and warehouses on navigable water. After the Revolution, cabinetmakers of Richmond, Alexandria, and other Virginia cities and towns began the factory-like production of furniture in the styles of Hepplewhite, the Directoire, Sheraton, and Empire, successively. The highest-styled "French antique" furniture —now called Victorian—was made for Virginia homes. Traditionally, they were willing to sacrifice older styles for this new vogue sparked by the Royal Restoration in France.

Baltimore, after 1785, shipped much excellent furniture to Virginia. The first glass furnace in America was set up at Jamestown, Virginia, early in that first settlement's history. An idea of the grandeur and opulence of a Virginia home of the early eighteenth century may be had from a visit to the restored governor's palace at Williamsburg. One visit to this spot will convince any skeptic that our top-drawer colonists lived as well, or better, than their peers in old England.

Chapter III

MASSACHUSETTS

IMAGINE, if you can, a religious commonwealth in which people are treated as children. The only adults recognized as such are the clergy. The "half-grown" are the elders who support the clergy, acting as spies on the consciences of the people. All activities of life, private and public, are supervised. All mankind in the commonwealth are sinners, destined for the fires of hell. Life must be spent in continuous repentance until the inner light tells you you are of the elect and ordained to be saved. This is Calvinism at its pinnacle—or its nadir—a religion so inspired of God that its penalty, for a child who struck a parent, was death. This pictures the Geneva experiment carried to America and known as the colony of Massachusetts Bay. This is the self-imposed handicap the Puritans donned as a halo, and by which they misdirected their energies for almost a century. Luckily, the still small voice of conscience and a sense of justice did not entirely die within the people who submitted voluntarily to this philosophy of life. Common sense survived. By the turn of the eighteenth century Massachusetts had saved itself.

It may be that Cromwell's holy experiment, the murder of King Charles I, and the unrestricted destruction of religious and secular antiquities and works of art in England caused some doubts even among those to whom doubt was but another word for damnation. During the

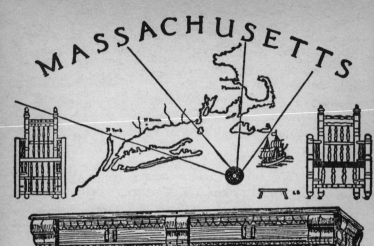

MASSACHUSETTS

**SERRATED CUPBOARD WITH BULBOUS UPRIGHTS
AND ARCHED CENTER PANEL**

regime of the Lord Protector, a gaming table and a stained-glass window in a parish church were in the same category of unholy things. A volume of Shakespeare was as much the work of the devil as a rubricated *Book of Hours*. People, ideas, manners, and things of orthodox nature were all tabu to Puritans—things to be destroyed on one's own pathway to heaven. Actually, the Puritans themselves were hardly to be blamed. Their self-delusion, as recorded in documented deeds and events, reads like an inferno of self-hypnosis. Until the people snapped out of their delusions, Massachusetts was in a fair way to breeding a thousand families such as the Jukes'.

Yet this is the backdrop of the stage upon which are posed the antiques of seventeenth-century Massachusetts. Luckily the stage had more than the backdrop. It also had wings. These were painted by an occasional minister who led his flock into more tolerant ways, by free-thinkers, by merchants, officials, and royal governors. Incidental scenery is also on the stage—scenery painted because of the natural unrest that bedeviled so many common people while the great experiment was acted out to its final end. New village after new village dotted the Massachusetts countryside as the seventeenth century rolled on. By this form of compensation people escaped from each other in groups. Each new village was less of a prison of the mind than the village from which the settlers had fled.

Massachusetts people, by and large, could have had fairly comfortable, livable homes by 1650. The trouble was, comfort and ease was a cardinal, or deadly, sin. Furniture was a necessary evil. What there was of it was there to stay. Never would the idea of supplanting it with something better and finer occur to the Puritan— so long as he remained a Puritan. The only destroyer of

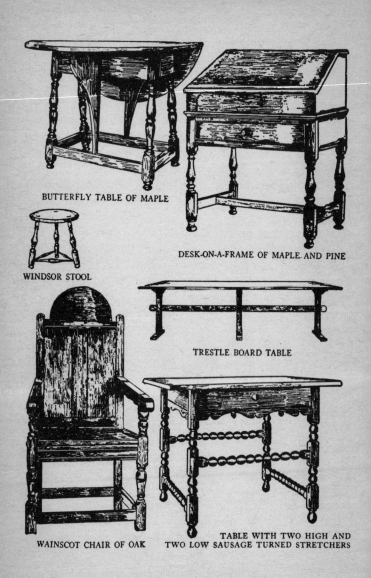

BUTTERFLY TABLE OF MAPLE

DESK-ON-A-FRAME OF MAPLE AND PINE

WINDSOR STOOL

TRESTLE BOARD TABLE

WAINSCOT CHAIR OF OAK

TABLE WITH TWO HIGH AND
TWO LOW SAUSAGE TURNED STRETCHERS

JOINT STOOL

HUTCH TABLE OF PINE

CRANE BRACKET
BUTTERFLY TABLE

ONE-DRAWER LINEN CHEST

CHEST-ON-A-FRAME WITH
SCRATCH CARVING

houses and furniture was fire. Because of faulty chimneys and general all-wood home construction, Massachusetts had lots of fires, otherwise we would no doubt have a great deal more of the furniture of the Pilgrims and Puritans available to us today as antiques. But they did have the fires. Hence early New England furniture was scarce even before the pursuit of antiques engaged the interest of the first collectors.

Massachusetts people enjoyed the following items: Hutch, stretcher, trestle, gate-leg, butterfly, and saw-buck tables. Turned and wainscot chairs. Settles, benches, and joined stools. Chests, hutches, Bible, and desk boxes. Beds, pallets, and "one-post" beds.

The gentlemen, merchants, officials, and governors, together with an occasional minister and scholar, had all these if they wanted them, plus these finer items: Drawing tables. Day beds. Upholstered chairs. Court and press cupboards, and perhaps even livery cupboards. Credenzas and other top-drawer Elizabethan furniture borrowed from Spain.

In the first category of pioneer things, maple and pine were the favored woods although some oak was used. Most of the stuff was made by joiners and arkwrights. In the second category, the touch of the cabinetmaker was mandatory.

When Cromwell's regime ended in old England, the Massachusetts Colony had impressed upon it the will of the restored Stuart line. The Puritans' houses of worship were used by the Church of England, despoiled and abominated by a hated form of religion that admitted all sinners had a fifty-fifty chance of getting to heaven.

Hellish new ideas in furniture, silverware, the painting of "counterfeits" of people (portraits), and other inventions of Satan entered the port of Boston. Even at this distance of time one can see the Puritans squirm. We can be glad they did. Out of the squirming emerged a new, revitalized people. Energies were redirected into constructive channels. Invention flourished. The blossoming of New England is something over which we, as Americans, can take great pride. The first fifty years of seventeenth-century Massachusetts was hell on earth for many people. Yet the descendants of those people turned it into a sort of heaven. By 1704 a newspaper was permitted publication in Boston. Portraits were painted after 1670, the most famous being those of Mrs. John Freake and her baby Mary, and of Mr. John Freake, merchant and attorney of Boston. Mr. Freake is posed dressed almost as a courtier. Mrs. Freake wears clothing rich and rare for that time and place.

The cabinetmaking craft flourished in Boston, perhaps from about the same year painters began making portraits. The new order was beginning. Money was being made, and spent. A new class of well-to-do artisans, as well as merchants and traders, was beginning to take over the job of keeping the Massachusetts brand of the New England conscience. Canopied beds, fancy mirrors, fine caned chairs and other elegancies, Dutch tea tables, damask-covered furniture, and comparable luxuries were advertised for sale in Boston during the first fifteen years of the eighteenth century. And so began the second hundred years. Fine things were imported before fine things were made generally by Massachusetts artists and artisans. When musical instruments for the people began coming in as merchandise, and when musical instrument makers set up their shops about 1720, we can be sure the stranglehold of Calvinism on Massachusetts was finally broken.

Silverware, an item detestable and unholy to the dyed-in-the-wool Puritan, came into favor because it was a very practical way of keeping one's silver money and

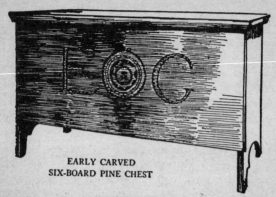

**EARLY CARVED
SIX-BOARD PINE CHEST**

HEAVY OAK BALL-FOOT CHEST WITH APPLIED MOLDING

PAINTED LINEN CHEST OF PINE

OAK CHEST SHOWING ARCHITECTURAL DETAILS

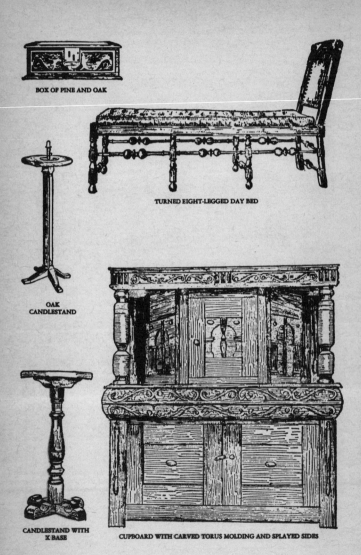

BOX OF PINE AND OAK

TURNED EIGHT-LEGGED DAY BED

OAK
CANDLESTAND

CANDLESTAND WITH
X BASE

CUPBOARD WITH CARVED TORUS MOLDING AND SPLAYED SIDES

ROUNDABOUT
CHAIR WITH CROSS
STRETCHER

EARLY OAK BIBLE BOX

PINE SETTLE

PINE LINEN CHEST

BANISTER-BACK SIDE CHAIR
WITH CARVED
TOP RAIL

using it too. By 1680 there was much silver coin circulating in Boston. The wise ones hired silversmiths to turn it into tableware and utensils. Thus began a silversmithing trade of no mean proportions which sparked the creation of much early American silver that is today collected by a company of stout-pursed people. The work of Coney, Dummer, and that smart businessman, Paul Revere, whether represented in a porringer, a teapot, or even a spoon, is worth several times its weight in pure gold or platinum.

Revere silver has an aura, a halo, of such proportions that any piece bearing his magic mark is worth two to ten times the work of contemporary silversmiths whose work, by and large, is better than Revere's. And not all silver marked "Revere" or even "P.R" is by the ubiquitous Paul the Patriot. Revere hired silversmiths to make unmarked wares for him which he stamped with his own name. He was not trying to hoodwink the public. He was doing precisely what certain jewelers do today, marking what he sold with his, and not the actual maker's, name. It is much to be doubted whether Revere was unique in this practice even in his heyday. Most of the silver marked Revere was made and sold after—not before—the Revolution. Revere lived to a great old age and was active up to the end of his life. The grand portrait of Revere, the working silversmith, painted by John Singleton Copley *c.* 1765, pictures the hero as a young man. Revere died in 1818. Between 1785 and 1815 the silverwares produced, no matter by whom, and bearing the Revere stamp, add up to a total that bespeaks the beginning of mass production. All of it is rare, precious, and worshiped today. The brass and copper business founded by Revere continued. The name of this man, made famous by a poem for children, is still stamped on the metal he turned to in making bolts, hard-

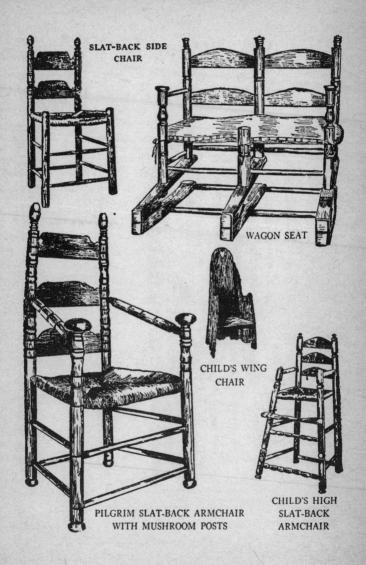

SLAT-BACK SIDE
CHAIR

WAGON SEAT

CHILD'S WING
CHAIR

PILGRIM SLAT-BACK ARMCHAIR
WITH MUSHROOM POSTS

CHILD'S HIGH
SLAT-BACK
ARMCHAIR

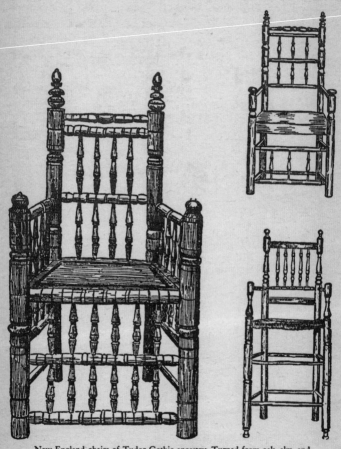

New England chairs of Tudor-Gothic ancestry. Turned from oak, elm, and
other woods, and now known as the Brewster and Carver type chairs. All
seventeenth century from *c.* 1650–1680.

ware, and bells for his beloved Boston and his home state of Massachusetts.

From the number of advertisments culled by George Francis Down from early Boston newspapers, we can, in our turn, know that much, very much, in the way of furniture, mirrors, clocks, chinaware, and similar objects were imported by Boston merchants after 1700. Perhaps many items heretofore considered made in Massachusetts were not made there at all. We can also be sure that Boston and other Massachusetts cabinetmakers used the imports as models for making similar things. After 1750 the Windsor or Philadelphia chair was made generally throughout Massachusetts. At Taunton, in the first half of the eighteenth century, a group of Huguenots made engaging painted chests that are today considered among the most desirable of Massachusetts antiques.

At this point it may be well to inject the antiquarian comments of a writer in the *United States Magazine* in 1856. This writer, in dealing with the chairs of the Pilgrims now known as Carver, Brewster, and Winslow types, said: "The passer down Broadway [New York] at almost any time may see an excellent revival of the Pilgrim chair at the store of Mr. J. C. Cummerford. They are well made, of seasoned oak, and are temptingly spacious and inviting; there is no doubt our Pilgrim families are ready to supply themselves with so good a model."

Thus did the first attempts at reproducing the early furniture of Massachusetts get publicity from a writer on antiques in 1856. If Mr. Cummerford, who is listed as a chairmaker from 1838, made his reproductions in the old manner, from well-seasoned oak—and there is every reason to believe that he did make the chairs well and good—then some of his production of almost one hundred years ago may now be cherished as originals of the seventeenth century.

The Willards, at Roxbury, developed that marvelous wall clock, the banjo, and patented it only to have it widely pirated by many other good Massachusetts clockmakers. Tall-case or grandfather clocks were made at many places. After the Revolution there were cabinetmakers of Boston and Salem whose work is today worshiped with all the reverence it deserves.

There can be no question about it. Massachusetts cabinetmakers produced lovely furniture and chairs in the styles now designated, respectively, as Georgian, Chippendale, Hepplewhite, and Sheraton. At Newbury, Stephen Jacques was working in the 1690s making furniture of oak in the style of William and Mary. In the period 1725 to 1740 Joseph Brown at Newbury was making very good Queen Anne-style and Georgian furniture. The Essex Institute owns his account book. Joshua and Abraham Lunt were making Georgian- and Chippendale-style furniture at Newbury from the 1730s to the 1770s. Their account books, also preserved, reveal a production that indicates sales made not only in Newbury but also in Boston. John Short, who began working as a cabinetmaker at Newbury in 1736, appears to have been the first of a trio who made fine furniture for almost a century. Joseph Short, working in that part of Newbury which finally became Newburyport, put labels on his product made in the 1790s to 1818. His label quenches for all time the allegation that the term "Martha Washington" for the high-backed upholstered chair with open wood arms is a modern appellation. Joseph Short called his chairs of this type "Martha Washington" on his printed label.

At Dorchester, Massachusetts, Stephen Badlam, who worked from the 1770s to 1815, made some very fine

Hepplewhite- and Sheraton-style chairs and cabinet furniture. Badlam branded his name on some of his chairs, perhaps most of them. His Hepplewhite-style furniture is today considered the peer of Baltimore Hepplewhite, which is saying a great deal.

At Dorchester, also, John Seymour and his son Thomas began making the furniture that today causes a hush to fall over the audience when an example of it is offered for sale at auction. Thomas Seymour established the Boston Furniture Warehouse from which fine cabinetwork by him and his father, and other cabinetmakers, was sold at retail and exported in some quantities to Southern ports. The Seymours' finest furniture is in the style of Sheraton. In fact, Seymour Sheraton chairs appear to be the only American-made Sheraton chairs that could be sold in England as true Sheraton. Other American cabinetmakers appear not to have followed Mr. Sheraton's own designs as meticulously as did the Seymours. Seymour secretary desks are exquisitely made. Almost all of them have the interiors painted a sort of robin's-egg blue. This is considered a Seymour trademark. It is also a feature that establishes the price mark of Seymour secretaries today.

John Doggett of Roxbury had a manufactory for the production of tabernacle and other types of mirrors from 1800 to 1830. Doggett labeled his mirrors. These, too, are now precious antiques from the state of the bean and the cod. It is believed that the Doggett label was used by his successors after 1830, perhaps to 1840. This is quite natural. Doggett had an enviable reputation, gained from his own production and distribution efforts. His label was as important then as is the label of any factory today.

Experts have at times commented on the fact that Massachusetts Chippendale furniture displays a restraint

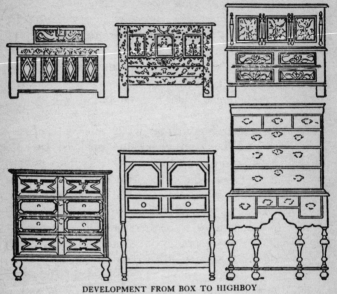

DEVELOPMENT FROM BOX TO HIGHBOY

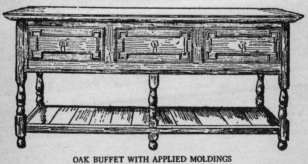

OAK BUFFET WITH APPLIED MOLDINGS

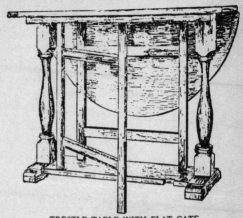

TRESTLE TABLE WITH FLAT GATE

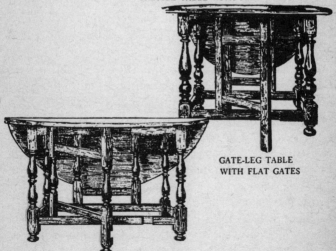

GATE-LEG TABLE
WITH FLAT GATES

GATE-LEG TABLE

unknown to the cabinetmakers at work in Philadelphia before the Revolution but that after the Revolution the furniture of Massachusetts appears to have thrown off all restraint. This is true. And it may well be that this throwing off of what might be characterized as "conservative influence" was caused by the making of furniture for export as well as home consumption. Also, after the Revolution numerous fine artisans, trained in the English tradition, emigrated to Boston. One of these, David Poignand from the channel island of Jersey, arrived in 1787. His work, produced in Boston, has the look of furniture produced by the best London cabinetmakers. Some furniture made at Boston, Salem, Dorchester, and Newburyport at the turn of the eighteenth century looks almost like Philadelphia furniture made four to five decades earlier. Some of it might well be attributed to Gostelow of the Quaker City.

At Salem, Jacob and Elijah Sanderson and Josiah Austin, all fine cabinetmakers, created a cartel for the production and sale of furniture. They were active from the 1770s, during the Revolution, and enlisted all the fine cabinetmakers of their neighborhood in their enterprise. And "enterprise" is the right word for what the Sandersons and Austin did about furniture production and sale. Mabel Swan, in her excellent monograph published by the Essex Institute, *Samuel McIntire, Carver, and the Sandersons*, calls the enterprise a "Furniture Trust Company." These men supervised the production of their own furniture and the output of many other shops, and shipped it by water to Southern ports— Charleston, Savannah, Saint Augustine, New Orleans, the West Indies, and even to South America. They made furniture to sell on sight. They studied their market. They realized their market wanted fine carved and in-

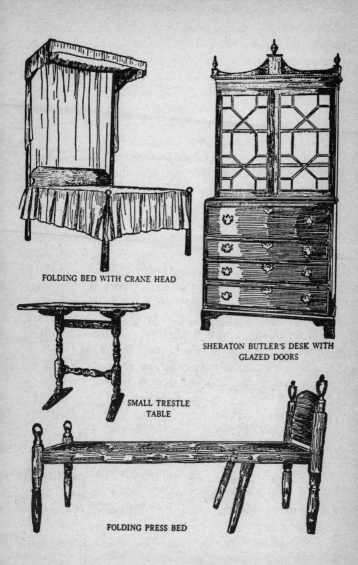

FOLDING BED WITH CRANE HEAD

SHERATON BUTLER'S DESK WITH
GLAZED DOORS

SMALL TRESTLE
TABLE

FOLDING PRESS BED

laid furniture, deep upholstery, fine fabrics—and they gave it to them.

Samuel McIntire, the famous carver, architect, and housewright, did work for this group. William Fiske, Deacon Adams, William Appleton, William Luther, William Hoock (or Hook), Francis Pulsifer, and Samuel Frothingham, all fine cabinetmakers, made furniture for this sales company. Daniel Clarke, Samuel F. McIntire, Micaiah Johnson, Jeddediah Johnson, Edmund Johnson, and the Burpee Chair Manufactory worked for this great furniture and chair "combine." By this activity some of the finest furniture ever made in America was distributed throughout Massachusetts and the South.

It would be nice to be able to say "all this furniture was in such-and-such a style and is readily identifiable." But it cannot be said, because this furniture, made between 1778 and 1812, embraced chairs in the Queen Anne, Chippendale, Hepplewhite, and Sheraton style, and cabinet furniture in the same styles. Geographically speaking, this furniture production and selling effort out of Salem extended Massachusetts furniture to all our coastal cities and towns, from which ports it was carried farther inland. No less than 600 pieces of furniture from the Salem enterprise were originally purchased in Florida, along the St. Johns River. Most of this, when found in 1914 to 1930 by antiques scouts, was purchased and shipped North again. Some of it went right back to Boston and Salem.

Strangely enough, there is evidence that either this Salem combine or a Boston trader whose name or identity is not yet revealed, also shipped "old and used" furniture to Florida in trade for grapefruit (then known as "shaddock") and other citrus fruits. This old and used furniture was, of course, "antique" at that time. The late C. W. Lyon found much of this furniture in the cottages of descendants of the Minorcans who, brought to Florida by a canny Scotsman planning to establish a little empire with the Minorcans as subjects, found them not so docile and had a revolution on his hands. The Minorcans stayed in Florida and traded their produce to Boston traders for Massachusetts antiques. On rare occasion there comes to light in and around Boston a bit of pottery that looks like Mediterranean ware. Chances are that that pottery is of Florida Minorcan make, traded along with citrus fruits for what were then considered the hand-me-downs of Massachusetts furniture.

RHODE ISLAND

Rhode Island John Goddard Block Front Furniture

Providence

BROKEN-ARCH BLOCK-FRONT CHEST-ON-CHEST

Chapter IV

RHODE ISLAND

RHODE ISLAND and Providence Plantations, to give the colony and state its correct name, was the first new and separate colony of New England. Religious differences within the ruling group which settled Massachusetts Bay caused the establishment of this colony which, from the very beginning, enjoyed a form of independence that soon became self-government. As the colony thrived, its towns of Newport and Providence increased in size.

The furniture made in this colony up to the first quarter of the eighteenth century seems to have remained well within the standard patterns that characterized the furniture of Massachusetts. When, however, Rhode Island cabinetmakers began working in the styles of William and Mary, and in the later Queen Anne and Georgian patterns, something happened. That "something" was the development of a style now known as block-front furniture, often called the finest and most distinctive furniture style developed in the American colonies.

Unfortunately we cannot claim the block-front idea as American. But we can claim the development of the style to a point of perfection undreamed of by those who first used it. Something similar to our block-front was developed in Venice and also in the Netherlands. The Venetian block-front is rococo. The Dutch style seems to be a variant of the William and Mary. It is likely that both the Netherlands and Venice got their block-front idea from the Chinese.

John Goddard, stylist and greatest exponent of block-front furniture, was born in Newport and became perhaps America's greatest individual craftsman. Although he did not originate this type of furniture, as many have claimed, he did develop it and carry it to perfection. His is the only American cabinetworker's name which is, with certainty, associated with block-front furniture.

The Chippendale influence that was overrunning the colonies at this time touched John Goddard but lightly and never completely dominated his personal expression and excellent craftsmanship. We may say his style was more substantial than Chippendale's, and surely more so than that of the imitators of the great designer who were working elsewhere throughout this country. Newport, even at this early date, was a wealthy seaport. Its luxurious homes were filled with imported and the best locally made pieces, the former of which no doubt often inspired Goddard.

The shop of Job Townsend, situated also in Newport, was the scene of Goddard's first activities. He worked there at an early age and in later years married Townsend's daughter. Sixteen children were born to them but only one followed his father's profession, and even this one never became a skilled craftsman. While working for Townsend, Goddard first attempted block-front furniture, but it was crude experimenting. In many of these early attempts we find that the block is very shallow, scarcely raised above the carcass of the piece, and that the shell motif is missing. In general, early block front lacked the refined finish that the later pieces boasted as one of their greatest charms.

Goddard produced many pieces of furniture without the block front. Let us take, for example, a highboy attributed with considerable authenticity to his workshop. In this example all influence of Chippendale has been swept aside and the graceful spirit of the Queen Anne predominates. In the rhythmic lines of the apron we find the shell motif swinging gracefully into a simple cabriole leg, but the general lines of the carcass of the piece, as well as most of the decorative detail of its embellishments, is of a period earlier than Chippendale. The base contains three small drawers side by side and above them a long drawer extending the full length of the piece. The top has three large drawers and above them, centered, a small square drawer with two smaller rectangular drawers flanking it. Above these is a large panel that follows in line and accents the broken pediment. A carved flame appears at either end and in the center of the arch. Plain brasses complete the piece, adding another note of perfect dignity.

As time went on Goddard, working at the block front, deepened the blocks and elaborated the shell carving, which so successfully counteracted the predominating perpendicular lines. When three blocks appear on his furniture the inner one is concave and the outer ones convex, with the shell c̆orresponding. Not only was this shell an integral part of the design, but the bracket foot was blocked, carrying the blocking treatment down through the molding into the foot.

An ingenious expression of Goddard's love of grace is seen in the rosette design at the arch of the pediment, which revolves and thereby leads the eye back along the flowing line of the pediment.

In Goddard's kneehole desks the center panel was set far enough back to make room for the knees when sitting before it, but the blocking was identical with that of the straight-front desks, or omitted in the center section and replaced with a plain panel. This panel was hinged

BLOCK-FRONT DESK

BLOCK-FRONT BUREAU

and, when opened, disclosed a row of drawers or shelves. Many of these desks were ornamented with pierced Chippendale handles which no doubt were imported from England or reproduced by local craftsmen to Goddard's orders.

In the tall desks of this craftsman strength and dignity prevailed, and the illusion of additional height was given by the repetition of the perpendicular line. A broken-arch pediment added still more to this effect. The door fronts of the upper section followed unerringly the blocking of the desk front and lid. The three blocks of the upper case are divided so that the left front hinges on the side of the body and the middle panel is hinged to the panel at the right, which was in turn again hinged to the right side of the body. This method of hinging was also reversed.

Candle pulls (small, flat, pull-out shelves) were added to these tall desks to furnish a place for lighting equipment. A half-round fluted column broke the severe line of the corners of the upper part and converging shells decorated the small drawers on the inside of the desk.

The finest block-front construction is characterized by blocking worked from sections of fine cabinet wood at least three inches thick. Which is to say the blocking —the cavities and the protuberances—is carved from a single piece of wood. In the less meticulous forms the blocks in many cases were applied and not carved from a solid piece.

It is interesting to note that Goddard, in spite of all his earnest efforts and skilled craftsmanship, died bankrupt. Now examples of his furniture bring among the highest prices paid for any American antiques. Unlike many cabinetmakers, he did not put labels on his furniture, which makes it difficult today to trace with authenticity actual examples of his handiwork.

GODDARD DETAILS

BLOCK-FRONT BROKEN-ARCH SECRETARY

Throughout Connecticut, Massachusetts, and New Hampshire we find examples of block-front furniture, some of which, no doubt, came from the Newport shop of John Goddard and some of which was certainly made by other unknown craftsmen who recognized the decorative possibilities of the block front and attempted to make it for their own clientele. In almost every case, however, they did so with less aesthetic success.

The details that Goddard employed in his furniture, as well as his foresight in creating unity and strength in the use of upright lines terminating in molded feet and the broken arch won him his laurels. This block-front furniture is the sufficient and enviable contribution of Rhode Island to the antiques of America.

CONNECTICUT

SUNFLOWER COURT CUPBOARD WITH
APPLIED CORBELS

Chapter V

CONNECTICUT

To MOST collectors, and to most students of American antiques, Connecticut spells chests, chairs, and clocks. Connecticut chairs and clocks are staples in the antique shops of this day, and staples in many collections. Connecticut chairs and clocks were originally made in such huge quantities that distribution was on a nationwide scale. The same, however, is not true of Connecticut chests. Excepting only press, court, and livery cupboards, the chests made in Connecticut and in the Connecticut River Valley are among the very scarcest items in the catalogue of Americana. Of course they are quite early. The dates of making seem to fall almost entirely within the last quarter of the seventeenth century, from 1675 to 1700. These chests have been posing problems of production source, provenance, and price since the first examples were rediscovered and recognized as rare antiques.

One important book, *The Hadley Chest*, by Dr. Clair Franklin Luther, and many essays and monographs, record the discoveries, conjectures, and ownership of these examples of pioneer furniture. Dr. Luther traces the distinguishing mark of the Hadley chest—cut and carved tulip and leaf decoration—to the Tyrol, to Norse designs, and to Celtic manuscripts. He ponders how these designs got to Connecticut and on Connecticut chests. He rather ruefully remarks that while the same designs appear a century later on Pennsylvania pottery, this doesn't help solve the problem of how they got to Connecticut.

Neither Macquoid in his *English Furniture* nor Foley in his *Decorative Arts* pictures a piece of English furniture carrying this tulip and leaf, or tulip-vine motif. But they could have. There is considerable early English furniture in private and public English collections on which this same basic design is cut. It is found on chests, cupboards, and chair backs of the early sixteenth century and seems to have gone out of favor at about the same time it became popular in the Connecticut Valley. Henry Shaw and Sir Samuel Rush Meyrick in *Specimens of Ancient Furniture,* published in London in 1836, picture a carved oak court cupboard with tulip-carved panels and other motifs found on our early American chests.

The present-day term, Hadley chest, was used by Luke Vincent Lockwood, Esq., in his *Colonial Furniture in America* to describe a chest in the Erving collection. He states that the chest was then (1901) known to collectors as the Hadley chest because many chests had been found in the neighborhood of that town. In Mr. Lockwood's opinion these chests originally were stained red, purple, and black. His opinion is quite soundly based on fact. Vestiges of staining, or original painting, seem to have been noted on every example thus far found. That some chests have been meticulously scraped and cleaned in order to display the original old oak is not proof that the pieces were not enlivened with color when made.

According to currently accepted proofs, the first Connecticut chest was made at Hartford by Nicholas Disbrowe who was born in England in 1613. He is said to have arrived at Boston in 1631, and moved to Hartford in 1639 where he was married in 1640. Existing records reveal that in 1660 he was given permission to erect a shop. Around 1680 Disbrowe is believed to have made the chest upon which is carved the legend "Mary Allyns Chistt Cutte and Joyned by Nich: Disbrowe." Some doubt has been expressed as to whether Disbrowe, coming to the colonies at the age of eighteen years, could have carried in his memory the designs he carved on this signed chest. Other conjectures seem to be that he might have been to Boston and saw there something like the designs he used. Up to now none seems to have considered the possibility of his copying, as best he could, designs from English furniture then owned in Hartford. Yet this is the most logical assumption of all. Traditions in respect of Connecticut chests once held they had come over on the *Mayflower* and succeeding colonial ships. Perhaps the traditions became a bit warped as they were passed down through the years. The original truth may well have been that these chests were *like* originals that had come over with the *Mayflower* and other early colonists' ships.

Of course it doesn't matter, except to serious students of social history, just how, or from what specific sources, Nicholas Disbrowe obtained his chest decoration patterns. He had them. He cut and carved them on one chest on which he also cut his name. In that one act he carved for himself a memorial more lasting than any ten tons of enlauding granite. Disbrowe, or whoever it was who made the first chest in the Connecticut Valley, started a vogue followed by other joiners. Other chest makers, now identified from contemporaneous records, include John Taylor of Hadley, Samuel Belding, and William and John Allis. Dr. Luther puts the surviving Hadley chests into two broad categories—the simon-pure type and the Hartford type. The Hartford type has split spindles applied as a part of the decorative scheme. The Disbrowe chest, made at Hartford, is not of this type. Structurally, the Hadley chest may have no drawer, or one, two, or three drawers. The more drawers the smaller the cavity under the chest lid. Four uprights, called stiles, stand at the corners of these chests and constitute the vertical framing pieces. The lower sections of these stiles continue downward to form the legs or stilts. Most of these stiles are flat boards carried down to the floor line without change in contour. Some, however, are square posts. When square, the stiles were usually lathe-turned at the bottoms to form the footing. The general construction scheme is three panels across the front and two to four panels at the ends. Most of the chests are carved all over the front—panels, stiles, framing, and drawer fronts. Some have only carved panels with grooved stiles and framing rails. On some others the stiles are plain, embellished with applied split-turned spindles. All of these chests are in the English tradition and no longer should there be any mystery as to the source of the designs used. They also came out of England.

In 1818, at the village of Barkhamsted, Connecticut, Lambert Hitchcock set up a little factory for the production of chair legs, chair rails, stiles, and back boards. It was his intention to manufacture these parts and to sell them locally in Connecticut and also to the chairmakers of Charleston, South Carolina, Savannah, Georgia, Chesapeake Bay ports, and conceivably also St. Augustine, Florida. Hitchcock's parts were purchased by chairmakers who assembled them, seated, painted, and decorated them, and thus were enabled to achieve production without the labor of turning and otherwise working lumber. His customers sold so many chairs assembled from Hitchcock's parts that Barkhamsted became a village of workmen's homes surrounding the Hitchcock factory. Business was indeed good.

CARVED HADLEY CHEST

CARVED CHEST WITH APPLIED CORBELS

Making chair parts had become so lucrative an undertaking by 1823 that Hitchcock conceived the idea of using his parts to make and market chairs under his own name. He then discovered the secret of his success lay in the ready salability of the chairs made from his parts.

The chief characteristics of the Hitchcock chair—almost standards because of his mass-production ideas—are two well-turned front legs with a nicely turned stretcher, a seat that is fairly wide at the front, narrowing in a graceful curve to the back, bent and shaped back posts which are an extension of the back leg, well-shaped back rails, rush seats, and stencil decoration.

Hitchcock not only stencil decorated his chairs on a straightline production basis but he also marked them through a stencil "L. Hitchcock, Hitchcockville, Conn." Barkhamsted became Hitchcockville all because of a chair factory. In 1826 a large three-story factory with cupola was erected. Children of his workmen were employed to paint the chairs, and wives and daughters applied the stencil decoration.

In 1829, because of the uneasiness of the times, Hitchcock went bankrupt, owing more than twenty thousand dollars. His assets included fifteen hundred chairs at the factory, fifteen hundred on consignment at New Haven, and many others on consignment straight across the country, all unsalable in the general business depression.

The receivers worked the business out of bankruptcy within three years. By 1832 it was again in full production with Hitchcock acting as sales agent and a former employee, Alford, serving as production manager. The chairs made after 1832 are stencil marked "Hitchcock, Alford and Company; Warranted." Business again boomed, but no longer did Hitchcock have a monopoly

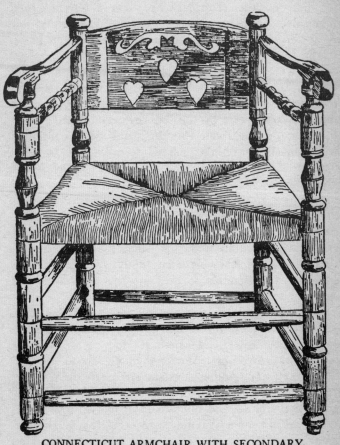

CONNECTICUT ARMCHAIR WITH SECONDARY
SAUSAGE TURNINGS AND HEART AND
CROWN DECORATION

in the fancy-chair business. Between his first success in 1823 and his bankruptcy in 1829 scores, yes, even hundreds of other chairmakers in other states concerned themselves with this simple question: "Why should our customers buy from Connecticut what we can make on the spot?"

Hitchcock had one advantage over most of the inland fancy chairmakers. He could ship by water throughout much of New England and New York State, and to Atlantic coast ports by the regularly established packet lines then in operation. The Hitchcock works continued to boom. In fact they boomed so well that by 1840 Hitchcock withdrew and in 1841 started another fancy-chair factory at Unionville, Connecticut, from which he shipped fancy chairs marked "Lambert Hitchcock." He continued making fancy chairs until he died in 1852. For thirty-four years this man had concerned himself with the production of but one item, the fancy, stencil-decorated chair. Knowing what we do of his production, it is not unreasonable to presume that in that period of years he produced a million fancy chairs!

It is reasonable to assume that Hitchcock got some ideas for the parts production of fancy chairs from the fact that as early as 1800 parts production for Windsor chairs was a general practice among wood turners. Extra spokes or spindles, legs and stretchers for Windsor chairs were on sale at most general stores and cross-roads emporiums. The Windsor chair had achieved such wide-spread production and use by 1800 that repairs became a household job rather than a matter of taking broken chairs to a chairmaker. Alpheus Hews of New Jersey may have been one of the Windsor chairmakers who introduced parts production to Connecticut. In 1786 this chairmaker located himself in Chapel Street, New Haven, where he began the production of Windsor

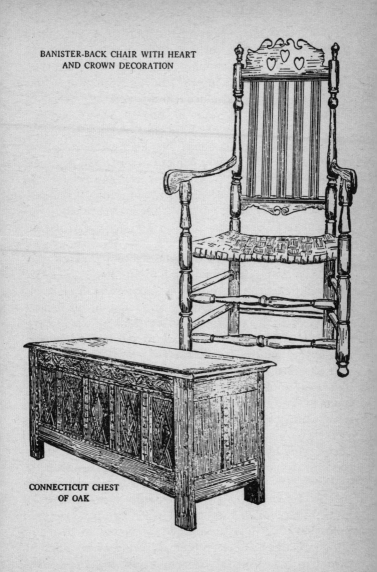

BANISTER-BACK CHAIR WITH HEART
AND CROWN DECORATION

CONNECTICUT CHEST
OF OAK

settees and garden chairs in a variety of fashions and traded his production for wet or dry goods and for any kind of timber useful to him in his chairmaking business.

In emphasizing Hitchcock fancy-chair production in Connecticut, it should not be assumed that Connecticut lacked production of chairs of other styles and periods. It may be said, however, that chairs of the seventeenth and eighteenth centuries made in Connecticut have few, if any, characteristics which mark them as unique.

Connecticut, however, is unique in clock production, because there were clockmakers in Connecticut who now appear to have had an entirely different approach to the problem of clockmaking and an entirely different philosophy of clock production and sale. We may well envision Simon Willard in Massachusetts concerning himself with the problem of how to build a timepiece of great perfection. If we turn to a Connecticut clockmaker of the early nineteenth century and judge of his mental activities from his recorded acts, his thinking would have been: "How can I make a clock to sell for ten dollars, and how many can I make?"

It is with the production of Eli Terry that clockmaking in Connecticut started on its royal road to becoming a national and international business. Terry developed an all-wood clock movement which he finally marketed in what is known today as the pillar-and-scroll case. This clock, every bit as lovely as a banjo clock, had something that the banjo did not have—capacity for variation. If you look at a banjo-cased clock and look at all types of banjo-cased clocks, it is easy to see that not over half-a-dozen variants of the basic design were possible. The pillar-and-scroll type case could be varied in so many different ways that no less than two hundred all different case designs finally evolved from it. Almost none of these variants was as delightful a case as the pillar and scroll.

It is now a moot question as to whether Chauncey Jerome, who in 1816 was working in the Terry case shop when the new patented one-day wooden movement was scheduled for casing, begged, borrowed, or just swiped the case design from Heman Clark. Clark used the pillar-and-scroll case before Terry. But Clark used the case to house an expensive all-brass, eight-day clock movement. Terry sold his clock, in a pillar-and-scroll case, for fifteen dollars.

Jerome, in his reminiscences as a clockmaker, speaks of changing over the Connecticut clock business from a wooden-movement to a brass-movement industry. The idea, he asserts, came to him in Richmond, Virginia, one night when he could not sleep because of worry over the depression of the times. Jerome made good on his idea, although the idea was neither original with him nor actually his property.

Another clock genius from Connecticut, Joseph Ives, had the low-priced brass-movement idea long before Jerome took it over and made a success of it. With his brass movements Jerome did what no other Connecticut clock manufacturer had ever done: he captured the English market. His brass-movement clocks would stand a sea voyage. Wooden movements couldn't be shipped by water; they swelled and wouldn't run. Jerome's clocks were sent to England at so low an entry price that the British authorities seized them at quoted value. They thought they were stopping a fraud. Jerome continued to send clocks, not caring whether a suspicious government or a satisfied dealer bought them. By the time his third shipment arrived at London the authorities knew that this Connecticut Yankee meant business.

It is impossible here to enlarge upon the wide variety of clocks made in Connecticut during the first fifty years of the nineteenth century, or to cover the earlier

BALL-FOOT LINEN CHEST

LINEN CHEST OF PINE WITH
SCROLL FEET

clockmakers who worked in this state and colony. Connecticut, as we have said, is famed for its chests, its chairs, and its clocks. The chests for which the state is famed are the ultimate in rarity. The chairs by Hitchcock have become a household word. The old Hitchcock factory is again in operation, making chairs in the same pattern and in the same way they were made more than a century ago.

The clocks of Connecticut, from the earliest to the latest even by courtesy called an antique, include just about everything imaginable: fine grandfathers, superlative grandmothers, two hundred all different mantel clocks, and enough cast-iron, bronze, and all-wood novelty clocks to satisfy the most exacting collector.

Among the nineteenth-century clockmakers of note whose products are today classified as antique are the following:

Eli Terry, Seth Thomas, Heman Clark, Silas Hoadley, Chauncey Jerome, Henry Terry, Silas Terry, Gideon Roberts, Joseph Ives, Chauncey Ives, Chauncey Boardman, Elijah Darrow, John Birge, Irenus Atkins, Elisha Manross, Butler Dunbar, Elias Ingraham, Alvan Wilcox, George Marsh, Solomon Spring, E. N. Welch, and P. T. Barnum.

It has been said that whenever a Connecticut clockmaker started a factory he actually founded five factories: his own, a case factory, and three others bound to be started by his original partners or master workmen. That's just about how clockmaking spread in Connecticut from 1800 to 1840. Millions and millions of clocks were made in these first four decades of mass production. Every clock made in this period is today collected as an antique.

Connecticut glasswares and other general items now classified as antiques will be found mentioned in succeeding chapters of this book. The major Connecticut story, as we have said, is wrapped up in chests, chairs, and clocks. The clocks of Connecticut are further commented upon in the clock chapter of this book.

Chapter VI

MAINE, NEW HAMPSHIRE, AND VERMONT

THIS northern tier of New England states is characterized by quiet, self-contained, and exceedingly self-reliant people. This has been the case since the region was first colonized. The winters are long, hard, and glorious. The summer seasons are air-conditioned by nature. The vistas are always grand. There are mountains, valleys, lakes, streams, passes, and, where there is ocean, there is also the seascape that has inspired—and awed—hundreds of artists. Maine enjoys the distinction of having been the site of the Popham colony on the Kennebec River in 1607. Thus Maine was probably the first spot in New England (or Northern Virginia as the section was then named) to have furniture of Elizabethan style. Maine became a state in 1802. Portland, first settled in 1632, came under the control of Massachusetts in 1658. Its name was then Falmouth Neck. In 1786 it was given its present name. Furniture was produced at Portland early in its history. The cabinet-making trade in the nineteenth century was extensive enough for conversion into factory operation. Early directories of Maine cities and towns include many names of potters, pewterers, silversmiths, chairmakers, cabinetmakers, and carvers. The shipbuilding industry in the early years employed the arkwright, that master of adze, ax, saw, and chisel, whose days were never idle. When there were no ships abuilding there was furniture to be made—good pioneer-type furniture in the old English yeoman tradition.

It is not beyond the realm of possibility that the ship-building ports of Maine, also functioning as trading ports, shipped furniture to Massachusetts towns. Certainly furniture from England came over to the ports of Maine, for wherever men acquired wealth in trade they imported furniture and elegancies from the homeland. Windsor and fancy chairmakers flourished locally in Maine. Only after antiques collecting became a national pursuit was Maine combed for its treasures. The first collectors were wealthy summer people who, seeking the quaint and the curious to give their so-called cottages an air of "belonging," began buying up the old furniture of the region. When the automobile began bringing thousands of tourists to Maine, its antiques began to leave the state. In 1927 a dealer in Memphis, Tennessee, had no less than one hundred pieces he had purchased in Maine the summer before. But were they actually Maine antiques? There was no proof. Most of the items had been purchased from Maine dealers who, in turn, may have purchased them in Massachusetts, New Hampshire, or in the province of New Brunswick.

New Hampshire has the unique experience of absorbing French styles from the north and Massachusetts styles from the south. In the northern part of New Hampshire one still on occasion finds a piece of locally made furniture showing certain elements of French influence. Twenty-five years ago considerably more French-influence furniture was found in northern New Hampshire than will be found today. The answer, of course, is that most of it has been collected.

New Hampshire was settled at Dover and Portsmouth in 1623, three years after the landing of the Pilgrims and seven years before the town of Boston was founded.

The first settlers were presumably fishermen, farmers, and traders. After the establishment of Dover and Portsmouth, Exeter and Hampton were the next settled places.

In the eighteenth century new ideas and styles in furniture entered New Hampshire from Massachusetts and, significantly, some of these seem to have traveled across Massachusetts from Rhode Island. The block-front style which reached its perfection of achievement in Rhode Island became a style that was favored—and modified—by the cabinetmakers of southern New Hampshire for a good many years. There is little carving on the knees of the New Hampshire block-front furniture, and in some cases it bears a closer resemblance to Queen Anne than to the Georgian style upon which block front was centered in Rhode Island.

It was quite natural that Dover and Portsmouth, because they were trading centers, would be the places where furniture of the so-called Pilgrim type would be known, used, and probably made for a good many years. But New Hampshire created no distinctive furniture styles, and it is doubtful if at any time it produced all of the furniture needed by its extending rural population.

New Hampshire's chief contribution to the furniture of America would seem to fall within the categories of its Pilgrim-era furniture and its block-front furniture made for the masses rather than for the classes. Certain local potteries operated in New Hampshire and many native chair factories of small output dotted the landscape after 1820. But these also produced furniture largely for local or within-the-state use. There is, however, record of considerable furniture trade out of Portsmouth between 1800 and 1810 and between 1816 and 1830. We cannot say for sure whether this furniture was produced

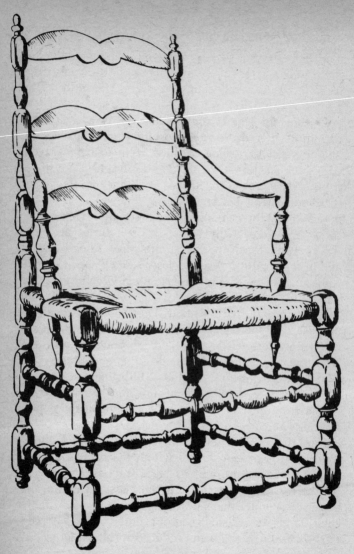

Salamander chair. The original of this chair was made in the French Jura as early as 1620. The style was carried to French Canada and from the Maritime Provinces slipped over the border, as a style, into Maine, New Hampshire, and Vermont. It is considered the finest slat-back chair in our Colonial scene.

in Massachusetts and used by Portsmouth shipowners as an item of trade, or whether the furniture was produced in New Hampshire.

The republic of Vermont, which was created out of the Hampshire grants, retained its identity as a separate "nation" until it applied and was admitted to the federal union, March 4, 1791. Many people consider Vermont one of the original thirteen states. This is an entirely logical assumption, because Vermont contributed tremendously to the winning of the Revolutionary War. The Green Mountain Boys who took part in that conflict were responsible for the great victory at Bennington.

A considerable Windsor chair output is traceable to Vermont. It is recorded that extensive Windsor chair factories were in operation at Keene, Fitzwilliams, and Bellows Falls. Many turners' shops in Vermont made Windsor chair parts, including legs and spindles, and other shops used these parts in the production of chairs. Every crossroads store and furniture shop sold Windsor chair "parts" either for home assembly or home repairs.

At West Randolph, Vermont, in the 1850s, the Salisbury Furniture Company began the mass production of a line of spool-turned furniture that included standard beds, trundle beds, cradles, worktables, and teapoys. About 1855 or 1856 this firm also produced standard lines of falling-front desks, cottage sinks, some with split spool-turned application, redolent of the early Pilgrim chests, and numerous other furniture items in a late Empire style. Also made in Vermont were thousands of four-leg dining tables with deep drop leaves fashioned of butternut, maple, and cherry.

In this northern tier of colonies and states French influence didn't merely filter across the Canadian border, it swarmed across, for from fifty to seventy-five miles "deep down" in Maine, New Hampshire, and Vermont we find unique chairs and tables which many commentators up to now have characterized as noteworthy American items. An example of this furniture is the "salamander" chair, so-called because it is a slat-back chair with the slats cut in the silhouetted form of salamanders, in pairs, meeting head on. The late Wallace Nutting, noting these beautifully shaped slats, the deeply turned legs and the beautifully molded arms, called it the finest of all American pioneer chairs. Actually it is French-Canadian. Of course the chairs were made in this country, but we did not develop the style. We copied it. Perhaps we made some improvements on it. One thing, however, is sure. None of us can say which salamander chairs were made on our soil and which were made in Canada. All we can be sure of is that they came to us from French Canada.

The Canadian table of this same family of fine, deep turned furniture was subjected to considerable improvement by the cabinetmakers and turners of the colonies and states here considered. We added upright finials to the crossed center stretchers and drops to the aprons. Other items of interest from Maine, New Hampshire, and Vermont will be mentioned in the special chapters which follow the geographic parade of states and colonies making up the forepart of this work.

Chapter VII

NEW YORK

WHEN the Dutch settled New Amsterdam and opened the North or Hudson River as far as Albany for trade, they planted seventeenth-century Dutch furniture styles upon Manhattan Island and in the Hudson Valley. These objects included general household furniture from the Netherlands and all refinements thereof deriving from Chinese motifs, acquired by trade, and Spanish motifs which had been impressed upon the Dutch during the Spanish occupation of the Netherlands.

Among the adventurers employed by the Dutch West India Company were many Swedes. A number of these took Dutch names and settled in the new colony. One, Olaf Svenson from Courland, a province of Sweden on the mainland of Europe, became known as the Courlander and changed his name to Van Cortlandt. The Van Rennselaers were also originally Swedes who had settled at Rennsellaer in the Netherlands and had changed their name to the Dutch Van Rennselaer. The Swedes in the Netherlands and the Swedes in New Amsterdam introduced geometrical forms such as circles, stars, and opposed hearts, which are often found carved on spoon racks and other items made in New York and Pennsylvania.

After the English gained control of the New Amsterdam colony, the Dutch influence continued and we see little change in either architectural or furniture forms

A DUTCH *KAS* WITH APPLIED MOLDING AND BALL FEET

until the turn of the eighteenth century. The William and Mary furniture which became popular in England toward the end of the seventeenth century was already in New Amsterdam. The style now known as Queen Anne, introduced to England at about the time the Queen for whom it is named succeeded William and Mary, was apparently known in New York before it was a popular style in England.

English cabinetmakers were working in New York throughout the eighteenth century. They made very fine furniture. But what they made is overwhelmed by the masterpieces produced in Philadelphia and by the block-front style developed by Goddard and others in Rhode Island. It required a revolution to develop an outstanding cabinetmaker in the Hudson Valley. But when that cabinetmaker did enter the scene, New York had its Duncan Phyfe.

At the close of the Revolution the people of the colonies suddenly discovered they had become a new nation. They had a feeling of what might be called cordial dislike for anything British, and an equally strong admiration for anything French. The result of this state of mind was the ready adaptation of prevailing French styles into everything used in the home; in clothing and furniture and even in architecture. When the French people, seeking precisely what we ourselves had just won, liberty and freedom, finally achieved them and established their Directory, they popularized the style known as the Directoire, based upon designs by the famous French artist, David.

This style has been called the most simple, the most lovely, and the most elegant furniture style ever designed. Its chief characteristics are the studied and resourceful use of the curved line. This is reflected at its best in chairs and sofas of great elegance and comfort,

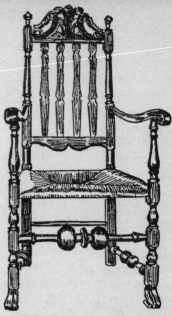

BANISTER-BACK ARMCHAIR WITH
SPANISH FEET, BULBOUS TURNINGS,
AND CARVED TOP RAIL

CARVED FLEMISH CHAIR WITH
CANE BACK AND SEAT

in graceful tables and stands, in bow-fronted cabinet pieces, and in beds and mirrors. The Directoire style could be used in the finest kind of expensive furniture and in the cheapest kind of common furniture. For rich or for poor, Directoire furniture was endowed with style rather than fashion. France did not long hold to the Directoire style. When Napoleon was made emperor in 1804, the Directoire style was rapidly replaced in France by the heavy neo-classic style known as Empire.

In New York, however, Duncan Phyfe made the Directoire style the guiding star of his own inimitable and masterful cabinetmaking. He permitted an after-glow of Sheraton and thus developed from these two specific styles a furniture that is the highlight of our early federal period.

Phyfe, a Scotsman by birth, came to this country with his family in 1784 at the age of sixteen, and settled near Albany. In that city he served his apprenticeship and later opened his first shop. Eventually the wealth of New York, already a growing metropolis, attracted him. In 1795 we find him established in Partition Street (later Fulton Street). Prior to this, he seems to have conducted a business in Broad Street and we know that he encountered many difficulties there before fortune brought his work to the attention of the John Jacob Astor family. Through their patronage, Phyfe eventually es-tablished a wealthy clientele. From 1810 to 1825 the peer of any and all American furniture came out of his shop. Original enough to warrant a separate classification, it lacked the bulk and artificiality of the Napoleonic pieces and retained all the grace and delicate charm of the Directoire and Early Sheraton. Line and proportion were excellent, carving and ornament were used with restraint, and all workmanship was unexcelled.

From 1830 until his retirement in 1847 Phyfe unfor-

WALNUT DESK WITH BALL FEET AND WELL

OAK PRESS WITH DROP PANEL

tunately fell to making the degenerate, overcarved furniture which persisted in America until the opening
years of the twentieth century. None of the articles made
during this period show any of his former excellence,
and we shall pass them by as the unfortunate effects of
a world-wide fad upon a cabinetmaker of some genius.

In 1837 Phyfe took his sons into the partnership and
the firm name became "Duncan Phyfe and Sons." By
1840 it was "Duncan Phyfe and Son," and remained so
until he sold the business in 1847. He died in New York
City in 1854, having lived a quiet, unpretentious life,
mingling rarely with his fellow men except when business demanded. He is known to have made an exquisite box in which bottles of water from Lake Erie
were sent to Lafayette as a souvenir of the opening of
the Erie Canal. Aside from this we can find no record
of public notice accorded him as an important figure
in the business life of the city. He did advertise in the
United States Directory for 1822, but paid only for listing his name as a cabinetmaker.

The social life of New York at the opening of the
nineteenth century was sophisticated and elegant. The
city was enjoying a period of great wealth and prosperity. Public taste was not fixed at a high tide of excellence, but was easily swayed by fad. Fortunately for
Phyfe, at this time his reputation had spread even to
neighboring cities, and orders poured in from the wealthier residents of New York, Boston, and Philadelphia.
Needless to state, as Phyfe's reputation grew and an
excellent patronage was assured him, his prices were cor-
respondingly increased. In fact, his prices of the period
are comparable to today's prices of well-made furniture.
We can judge well the extent to which his business had
grown by the fact that at the height of his career he
occupied 33, 34, and 35 Fulton Street, and had in his

CABRIOLE-LEG TABLE WITH SCROLLED APRON

OAK TABLE WITH TRUMPET TURNINGS AND GATE
LEGS IN THE FRAME

employ more than a hundred cabinetworkers and carvers.

The distinguished character of Phyfe's furniture resulted from his remarkable ability to combine the best elements of Directoire with the styles of late Georgian designers without sacrificing one to the other. In accomplishing this he achieved an originality of design which, coupled with excellence of execution, lifted him from the rank of everyday craftsmen to the height of his profession.

It has been said that more pieces of authenticated Phyfe furniture exist than of any other American maker, and although not all of what is attributed to him was made by him, his philosophy permeates them all. His fame we may justly attribute to his conceptions as a whole or to his restrained use of exquisite ornament, whether carving or veneer. In Phyfe's case veneer, although we may not observe it at first glance, was one of his chief elements in obtaining certain decorative effects. In general, all of his pieces are rectangular in shape, but less bulky and cumbersome than the prevailing continental mode.

Chairs and tables are probably the most representative pieces of Phyfe furniture although the sofas, beds, sideboards, and bureaus made in the Fulton Street shop, no doubt on special order to match chairs and tables, bear the stamp of his genius. In the earliest of these pieces it is not unusual to find plain turned legs, although the leg that we recognize as distinctly characterizing Phyfe furniture was concave, ending in a brass lion's foot or carved wooden dog's paw, and ornamented at the knee with acanthus carving.

In general structure and style Phyfe's chairs are all similar but in decorative detail they vary greatly. The front legs are curved forward and the back legs swing in a backward curved line from the top rail to the floor.

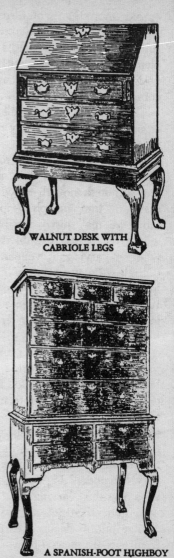

WALNUT DESK WITH CABRIOLE LEGS

A SPANISH-FOOT HIGHBOY

HIGHBOY WITH BROKEN ARCH AND QUEEN ANNE LEGS

Arms also begin at the top rail and run in deep curves to the arm support, which is scrolled, carved, or turned in an urn shape.

In the side chair we find a single line carried from the top rail into the line of the seat and often continuous down the front leg to the floor. Arms, the front of the back posts, front legs, and seat rails are reeded or carved with the acanthus. The broad panel of the back displays carved oak branches, wheat ears, thunderbolts, or cornucopias. Backs have the lyre-form splat, curved cross rails, or solid shaped horizontal panels.

These elements we find more or less combined in all Phyfe's chairs. Front legs may be round and carved and back legs square, and in many cases the front legs are straight and the back curved. No definite rule seems to have been applied to such constructions, although because the front legs alone were carved we find that their forms vary greatly, as those of the back legs do not.

The chairs fashioned after the curule seats of Rome made in Phyfe's shop are typical of the French Empire influence. The legs consist of double reverse curves crossed in the center and ending in brass lions' feet. Of this style two distinctly different examples exist. In one the back legs are identical with those found in the cross-rail chair and at the front the curved curule legs appear. The other has the curved legs at either side connected by a center stretcher. At the crossing of the curved legs appears a small carved medallion.

Some of the chairs made by this craftsman have caned seats but most of them are upholstered over frames which are set into the seat rail. In still others, and in many of the sofas, the upholstering is put directly onto the seat rails. On a few sofas the front rail is concealed by the upholstery.

Crossbars appear both doubly and singly as well as

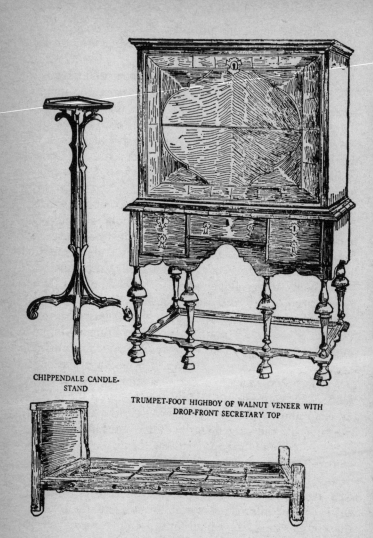

CHIPPENDALE CANDLE-
STAND

TRUMPET-FOOT HIGHBOY OF WALNUT VENEER WITH
DROP-FRONT SECRETARY TOP

TRUNDLE BED

curved and straight. A small rosette is placed where they cross and almost without exception they are reeded. Shaped horizontal splats consist of a small medallion or rectangle, uncarved and supported by carved scrolls. In a few of these splats the medallion is veneered. The lyre, as it appears in chair backs, sofa backs and arms, and table supports, is carved of wood, beautifully decorated with the acanthus. The strings, either four or five in number, are of brass or whalebone and the pin which runs through the top is of ebony. When the lyre appears on tables it is heavier and less delicately carved. Reeding appears on practically all Phyfe furniture. The front face of the back supports, often the top of the seat rail, particularly when it is continuous with the back line, and the front legs are all, in nearly every case, reeded. Occasionally front legs are carved with the acanthus or the dog foot which reaches half of the way or more up the leg to join the more conventional upper member.

The acanthus appears on the lyre in combination with parallel reeding, and in some instances on fronts of chair legs. Unlike his predecessors, Phyfe's acanthus consists merely of a series of grooves and ridges extending from a long center ridge which runs the entire length of the leaf.

Armchairs and sofas to correspond with all types of chairs were made in Phyfe's workshop. A few footstools exist which warrant the belief that they, too, were made to complete sets of drawing-room furniture. The arm-chairs show strong Sheraton influence with straight taper-ing legs and a predominant feeling of straight lines in their construction. The top rails of sofas are usually paneled in three or four rectangles, each or one of which is carved. The reeded arms curve from the top rail in an outward swing and end in a small scroll which rests upon a baluster with reeded shaft and carved urn. Front

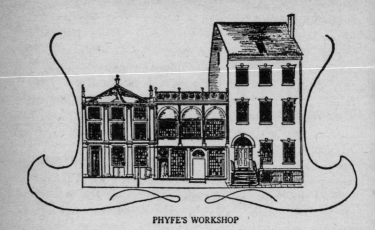

PHYFE'S WORKSHOP

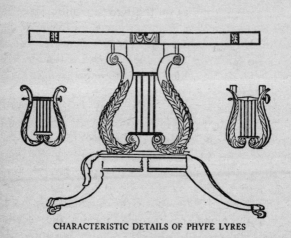

CHARACTERISTIC DETAILS OF PHYFE LYRES

and side rails display parallel reeding unless, as in some cases, the former is covered by the upholstery. Nearly all of these sofas are upholstered on back, arms, and seat, or have cane panels set between rails and uprights.

Although the curved-leg Phyfe chair is comparatively well known, few sofas of this type have survived. There is one exceptionally beautiful example in the American Wing of the Metropolitan Museum, New York City. This piece displays two exquisite lyre splats set in either arm. The top rail of the back as well as that of the arm is straight. The armpost sweeps in a continuous line into the seat rail and is reeded. Another sofa of this type has paneled rails, and lions' feet terminate the legs, which are carved ornately and join the seat rail in a large outspread eagle's wing.

Of Phyfe tables there is an overwhelming variety: the four-legged type with or without drawers and shelf; those supported on a center pedestal, such as a lyre or urn; and a third type fashioned after the trestle table and supported at either end by a lyre or coupled *colonnettes*. A few card tables of Phyfe origin exist with the fifth leg swinging out at one side to hold the extended leaf. These tables reveal Sheraton influence.

In this first general style of table Phyfe employed with great delicacy the best details of the Sheraton period—tapering reeded legs and characteristically turned small members. The legs above the turned portion are reeded and run up into a long block into which the skirting is set. Tops are square or rectangular, with oval, scalloped, or Pembroke corners. Drop leaves are occasionally used at either side or singly in the back, as in the case of the card table. Sometimes the skirting is plain and at other times paneled. In a few examples a small rectangular panel appears on one side only and is carved with drapery swag or leaves. The top block of the leg often dis-

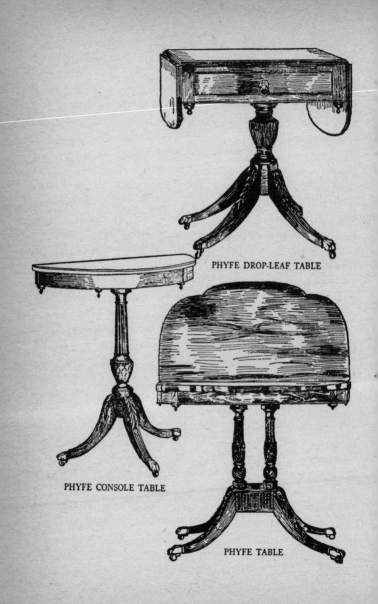

PHYFE DROP-LEAF TABLE

PHYFE CONSOLE TABLE

PHYFE TABLE

plays minute inlaid rectangles with square or oval tops. This particular inlay seems to have been representative of the exquisite detail Phyfe put into all his work.

With the addition of two small drawers or one large drawer or both and a shaped shelf set between the legs just above the feet, we have the Phyfe serving table. On this table the corners of the case are set into a fluted three-quarter column which is a continuation of the leg. The top curves out over the leg at each corner.

The second type of table, so beautiful from the hands of Phyfe and often enormously bad from the hands of his less gifted imitators, consists of a small platform upheld by three or four concave legs and supporting above it a center shaft of a single turned column or the lyre, as the case may be. The single shaft usually consisted of an urn, carved with the acanthus or reeded, and above it, supporting the top, a reeded or turned column. The concave legs bore acanthus carving, or reeding, or both. The platform, rectangular or round in shape, was also reeded at the sides. A brass lion's foot terminates each leg. In the case of the lyre shaft the platform is always square or rectangular. The lyre is carved with the acanthus, or reeded, and in general follows the construction of the lyre that was used in chair backs.

A console card table with a center shaft has an unusual inner mechanism that, when the leaf is raised for use, automatically throws the third concave leg out of line to form a perfect tripod. A few tables of this same period have center shafts composed of coupled colonnettes which we shall describe in detail later.

Both of these types appear in the extension drop-leaf dining tables and in similar dining tables of smaller dimensions, while the third and last type is confined almost entirely to library and dressing tables.

In this group coupled colonnettes or the lyre are sup-

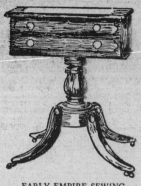

EARLY EMPIRE SEWING
TABLE

PHYFE LYRE-BACK CHAIR

PHYFE SINGLE AND DOUBLE CROSS-RAIL CHAIRS

ported on rectangular platforms at either end of the table. From two sides of the platform extend concave legs. Usually one or more drawers are set into the skirt and a delicately shaped stretcher or small shelf runs between the platforms. The colonnettes are light and beautifully turned while shelf and table edge are reeded or carved. Corner blocks often end in small finials or have small rectangles of inlay in decorative patterns set on each of the outer faces. Occasionally within a small paneled rectangle on the skirt a drapery swag or branches are carved. As in the chairs, we find many variants in Phyfe's tables that fall into two of these groups rather than consistently into one.

Beds of the four-post variety are attributed to Phyfe and in general are characteristic of those of Sheraton and Hepplewhite. Usually they are high and made without a footboard and with a very low headboard. The feet are turned and run up into a rectangular block from which rises a carved urn supporting a fluted column. The urn is sometimes carved with the acanthus and at other times reeded. In the latter case the acanthus appears at the base of the column below the reeding. At the head of the column is carved an adaptation of the palm-leafed capital that we find in Egyptian architecture. Other decorations include carved drapery forms and wheat ears. The sleigh or gondola bed appears later, and although the curved line of head and footboards might lead us to term it Duncan Phyfe's style, we can attribute not a single example of this type to his manufacture.

A Phyfe sideboard is extant with thin reeded and carved legs, center arched panel with a drawer above, and large doors at either side. This piece boasts beautifully veneered borders on drawer and door fronts as well as around the top.

Piano stands, dressing glasses, and buffets follow in general the characteristics that we have attributed to Phyfe, but all of these are rare.

Phyfe depended upon his wood for decorative effects; the results he obtained through the use of veneer are unique in the annals of American cabinetwork. Minute borders around corner blocks of tables, and wider borders about drawer fronts, at the lower edge of skirtings and along the sides of table tops are all characteristic of the care which Phyfe exercised in making the minutest detail beautiful. All of the veneer was made of carefully selected woods, usually crotch or curly mahogany, and by matching, juxtaposing, or contrasting the grain of the separate pieces he procured remarkable decorative effects on small and large surfaces. Phyfe also excelled in his carved ornamentation. The demand for fine materials was a result of the increasing wealth of the city and the growth of a complicated system of social life, with attendant cultural elements. In his furniture, Phyfe interpreted this affluence with a cautious restraint that ever kept within the bounds of refined taste.

The European elements, first French and later British, as the vogue demanded, appear in his work but never overcome his own sense of proportion. To him we may credit the fact that American Empire furniture far excelled that of both France and England, and for many years stayed far above the banal and ugly monstrosities into which the European styles fell within a few years after their inception. Carving as used by this master craftsman is always low in relief and unaffected in its simplicity, and next to his use of veneer may be said to be the most characteristic element of his work.

Until 1830 Duncan Phyfe avoided the mounting wave of garishness. Then he succumbed, along with the rest.

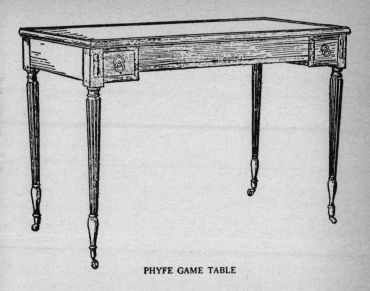

PHYFE GAME TABLE

PHYFE DROP-LEAF TABLE SHOWING SHERATON INFLUENCE

Came the period that we designate as Late Empire. This period lasted but a short while. Then came the rage for the "French antique" style furniture we now call Victorian. At times, of course, in the great quantity of furniture produced (never were homes more overfurnished) we are bound to find a flare of grace and beauty, but on the whole the period was marked with banality and artificiality. Furniture assumed monstrous size, with pompous and vulgar carving and no grace of line to redeem it. What few Sheraton details remained were so magnified as to become hideous. All ornament was cumbersome and brutal. In fact, little can be said for Phyfe's later period aside from the fact that workmanship still remained of the best.

Napoleon, in his spectacular career, was the only individual ever to dictate a period style and see it carried out. The success of this unnatural style for a while may be attributed only to the fact that Napoleon had at his command the greatest group of craftsmen and artists then living. Any furniture style not a direct outgrowth of the sentiments, aspirations, and lives of the populace at large is, at its incipience, false, and destined to a rapid death.

With the passing of a few short years, decadent tendencies crept into the French furniture, and American craftsmen, depending upon foreign inspiration, did little else than magnify these undesirable qualities. Not all the blame for what followed may be laid to France, for taste throughout our country was at low ebb and the work of conservative designers was not acceptable to the people. And, too, water power, which had been the mainstay of local cabinetworkers, was replaced by steam, and machines were invented which did the work of many carvers and turners in a fraction of the time that was formerly required. Quantity production ruined qual-

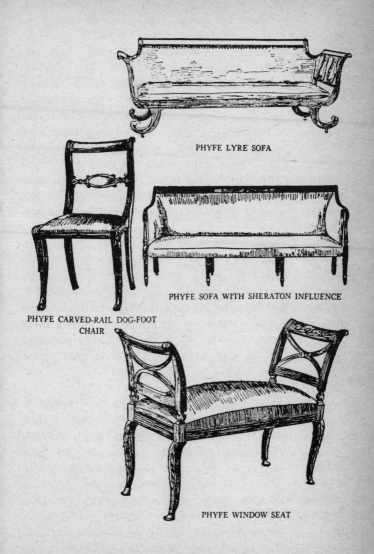

PHYFE LYRE SOFA

PHYFE SOFA WITH SHERATON INFLUENCE

PHYFE CARVED-RAIL DOG-FOOT
CHAIR

PHYFE WINDOW SEAT

ity. The clipper-ship period saw the building of our merchant marine and the opening of a great market for furniture that had not existed before. Manufactories could depend upon far-distant as well as local consumption, and the output was automatically increased to meet these demands. Handcut veneer was replaced by machine cut, and the chief beauty of this decorative method was lost. The pendulum had swung, but unfortunately too far, and nearly a century was required to rid the country of the miscreated results.

In actual furniture pieces it is a simple matter to trace the elegant qualities of Phyfe, the Empire, and Sheraton to their decadent stage. Sideboards probably show more clearly than any other pieces the results of enlarging and overcarving. The fronts remain severely straight or curve slightly and contain three or more drawers with cupboards below. This construction automatically brings the case of the piece nearer the floor and the slender legs of the earlier examples are replaced with massive, round, carved, or twisted pillars, terminating in a lion's or bear's foot realistically carved. The piece has become massive in general appearance and when slight ornament is applied, as in some cases, its beauty is overwhelmed by the bulk of the carcass.

Curves, wherever they appear, are too broken by carving to carry as continuous, graceful lines. This is particularly noticeable in table construction. We find clumsy bases, turned, carved, or gadrooned, with exaggerated thick concave legs. The pineapple and acanthus carvings are placed, not too sparingly, upon the center support, which rests on plinths, supported by carved ball-and-claw feet. In a few cases we are bound to recognize a certain dignity in this type of table but more often we are too conscious of the overambitious carver to perceive what beauties may lie hidden.

As time passes, every surface is veneered—on sofas, chairs, and tables. Bureaus sport swollen curves at either side, with the small top drawers occasionally following the line of the curve but more often recessed behind it. A scrolled panel or straight piece of wood is placed at the back of the top, and eventually small drawers are added to this construction. Enormous round wooden or glass knobs serve as pulls. Dwarfed, carved, and twisted pillars form the legs, and sometimes ornately carved thick columns break the corners.

One of the greatest changes the Empire period produced was in the size and form of beds. From the pleasant, slender dignity of Sheraton and Hepplewhite they became overpowering in thickness and confused with carving. To counterbalance this added weight, the posts became very tall.

A great change in interiors took place as a result of this heavy furniture. Homes, of necessity, increased in size, with the furniture as a scale rather than the human figure. A peculiar lack of sensitiveness to proportion appears in the fact that chairs never increased in size as did the other furniture but seemed, if anything, to become smaller.

It is unfair to call this entire period bad. Much of the carving, although overlarge, was exquisitely wrought, and the characteristic details employed in it—the laurel leaf, horn of plenty, and gadrooning—were in themselves beautifully proportioned. And yet the entire finished effect was that of a conglomerate mass of poorly arranged details, each calling for first attention.

To carry the development of furniture into the carved rosewood era would be to bring this record down to a time within the actual memories of many of us, so we will stop at the Late Empire and leave the Victorian period to speak for itself.

Not all the furniture made from 1830 to 1860 was bad. There were many high lights, yet the shadow caused by misdirected skill and taste deepened until many of the pieces of furniture became monstrosities of design and color.

We often speak of the horsehair furniture with disdain because somewhere back in our minds we have the mental picture of the poorly designed and overcarved frames. But let us not forget that many of the fine pieces that were produced before the Revolution were covered with horsehair.

So much has been written about Phyfe that any reasonable collector is justified in wondering whether or not the man and his work have not been overemphasized and overpromoted. To say that Phyfe's furniture is superior to that made in the same styles by the master cabinetmakers of Philadelphia, Baltimore, and Boston is to overstate, and consequently to decry, Phyfe. He did not do better work than these men. He simply did more. Whether we like it or not, Phyfe had a furniture *factory*, and his production was considerable. This overemphasis on Phyfe reminds one of the famed naval technique of the seventeenth century. Captains were concerned with coming to grips, achieved by tossing grapnels at each other's ships, tying the ships together, and slugging it out on board. "Throw out the grapnels and pull hard on the one that strikes" was the order of the day. Someone, looking for a great cabinetmaker in New York, threw out the grapnels and found Phyfe. Without sanding one bit from the patina of Phyfe's name and work we now know he deserves the crown of New York mastership for only a brief twenty years of our nineteenth century. Other cabinetmakers of comparable stature worked in New York City and in New York State.

The furniture made upstate, in Cherry Valley, displays

adaptations of the block-front style. Ball-and-claw-footed desks and chests of drawers and many other fine items were fashioned from cherry, maple, and mahogany. Further down in the Mohawk Valley, around Albany and at other points, another style of furniture was made—Shaker furniture. Perhaps we shouldn't say "style" in connection with Shaker workmanship. The Shakers certainly would not have called it a style. Shaker furniture is simple, functional, and ultra-conservative. This very philosophy of furniture making is now glorified in what is called Swedish Modern and, unfortunately, there are many advocates of this style who prefer it because of its "attempt" to escape from the antique. They just don't know what it is all about. Most Swedish Modern isn't modern at all. It is a re-creation of an antique style. Dutch influence on the furniture of New York is found reflected in the *kas*, or great standing chest with ball feet, in William and Mary and Queen Anne styles. Also found in New York are simple painted chests reminiscent of those found in Pennsylvania, and slat-back, fiddle-back and yoke-back chairs springing from original Dutch styles. There is little of the so-called Brewster or Carver influence at work save in the thin strip east of the Hudson.

In upper New York State the same sort of furniture Phyfe made in New York City was made by scores of cabinetmakers. They made what is considered Phyfe's best style of work for from five to ten years after Phyfe had stopped making it and had turned to what he, himself, designated as "Butcher Furniture." Not until about 1840 did the upper New York, or rural, cabinetmakers turn to Empire styles. Their excursion was short-lived. By 1845 most of them were making furniture in the new antique style now called Victorian.

Chapter VIII

NEW JERSEY

THE Netherlands, in making her bid for national expansion in America, located her principal New World port and trading post on the island of Manhattan. Dutch navigators explored the coast from that point south to the Capes and into the bay and river which they named the "South." New Jersey, entirely surrounded by water on three of its sides, was considered an island. Cornelius Jacobson Mey, for whom Cape May is named, was the principal navigator in the Dutch explorations. By what was called discovery, and by sparse occupancy, the Netherlands laid claim to the soil of these new lands. Dutch farmers and traders were early settlers in what are now Hudson and Bergen counties. By 1650 Dutch colonists had crossed New Jersey and were establishing settlements along the Delaware River. They crossed the Delaware into New Sweden, populating the Hoarkill Valley.

During this period the Netherlands' great continental rival for supremacy as a world power was Sweden. The Swedes completely disregarded the presence of the Dutch in New Jersey and established settlements from Cape May northward to above Millville. These, in fewer numbers than the Swedes on the west bank of the Delaware in what is now Delaware and Pennsylvania, nonetheless dominated southern Jersey at least until 1660. By 1664 Charles II of England, realizing that the Dutch had established a barrier between New England and Virginia, granted all the Dutch colonies of New Amsterdam and what is now New Jersey to his brother, James, the Duke of York. The Dutch at New Amsterdam capitulated to an English naval expedition in 1664. With the fall of New Amsterdam came also the fall of what is· now New Jersey. The Duke of York bestowed its proprietorship on John Carteret. The colony was named the Island of New Jersey in memory of the gallant defense of the Channel island of Jersey by Carteret against the forces of Cromwell in the English civil war.

Carteret, as proprietor of the new British colony taken from the Dutch by what might well be termed sheer piracy, established a policy to attract settlement and thus exploit the natural advantages of the colony. He offered a liberal form of government and free or low-priced land. He encouraged settlement by people from New England, and achieved it. Before many years the eastern portion of New Jersey was almost a counterpart of New England. In 1676 the colony was divided into eastern and western Jersey. Carteret's original colonists retained control of eastern Jersey while western Jersey became a settling point for Quakers. In 1676 this part of the colony was opened to all English Quakers desirous of coming to America. One of the important figures advocating the exodus was William Penn, who later obtained a colony of his own west of western Jersey.

New Jersey's settlement was planned for widely separate communities and intervening large plantations similar to those of Maryland and Virginia. In 1673 Jersey was recaptured and occupied by the Dutch who, incidentally, also recaptured New Amsterdam. The Dutch nation was finally granted the colony of Surinam in South America in exchange for its claims on New Jersey and New York.

The Duke of York became King James II of England—a monarch more thoroughly hated than his father, Charles I. He was eventually deposed and was replaced by William of Orange and his consort Mary. An English king, who, as the Duke of York, had stolen American colonies from the Dutch was replaced on the English throne by a Dutch sovereign.

This background history of New Jersey should indicate that northern New Jersey enjoyed furniture in the Dutch styles, New England-type furniture on its Atlantic coast, Swedish and Finnish furniture in the south, and English furniture on its western border, the Delaware.

There were, of course, many cabinetmakers at work in the northern New Jersey towns which, after 1700, began to develop with a rapidity comparable to the towns in New York, New England, and Pennsylvania. It is unquestionably true that northern New Jersey was continually influenced in terms of style by New York, and central Jersey influenced by Philadelphia. Southern Jersey continued using the pioneer-type furniture introduced by the Swedes and the Finns, culminating in the development of rush-bottom chair production on a large scale. This continued until at least the year 1900. Thousands upon thousands of slat-back chairs with rush seats, many made by the Ware family, were produced in southern Jersey and sold in Jersey, Pennsylvania, and Delaware.

In south Jersey we find the Swedish and Finnish panel chests which, in Pennsylvania, finally evolved into what is now called a Pennsylvania-German dower chest. It was a type of chest that appealed to the German immigrants, who found in it an ideal, all-purpose piece of furniture—a chest in which to store clothing and bedding, the top of which could be used as a table, and occasionally as a seat. At times two chests, end to end, also made a bed. The term "dower" as generally used is also a misnomer. Dower is a widow's portion. Probably what the users of the term mean to convey is "dowry" or marriage portion chest.

Eventually New Jersey had many men who produced fine furniture but they were overshadowed by the Philadelphia cabinetmakers Gostelow, Savery, and others, and by Phyfe of New York. These famous cabinetmakers were the fashion dictators of their day. It is natural that imitators of their work should appear in Jersey. It is not surprising then that we find, for example, labeled furniture by Matthew Edgerton of New Brunswick, New Jersey, who produced fine pieces in mahogany and cherry. He was noted for his chests-on-chests and his cabinets-on-chests. These were well designed, bracket-footed, with molded edges on the drawers. The top section contained cabinets of drawers which were topped with fine moldings. This furniture found its place in the prosperous homes in Jersey, and yet in the same towns distinctively styled Jersey as well as Pennsylvania farm furniture—round about Windsors and benches, tables, and bureaus—was used. Many Jersey chairs were similar to those of Pennsylvania. Decoratively turned finials at the top with narrow ribbon-shaped slats distinguish a Jersey-type chair. The armchairs had a flat arm, with a rolled front. These chairs seem a little too wide and too low. An over-size ball stretcher appears in the front of many of them.

Many of the roundabout chairs were made in comb-back style using spindles terminating in shaped head-pieces.

Jersey, of course, is famed for its glasswares, which are mentioned and discussed in a later chapter.

Chapter IX

MARYLAND

CATHOLICS, more or less convinced that Church and State are incapable of mixing, came to the religious-freedom colony planted for them by Lord Baltimore. They were happy to know that Maryland was not only a refuge for them but that Presbyterians, Episcopalians, and all other denominations were welcome.

Annapolis was the chief city of the Maryland colony until the establishment of Baltimore in 1730. The first settlement, however, was made at Saint Mary's, named in honor of Henrietta Maria, wife of Charles I. It is perhaps significant—in terms of respect for ancient things—that the capitol building at Annapolis shares, with the State House at Boston, the distinction of being one of the only two state capitol buildings now in use dating from pre-Revolutionary days. The first capitol building of Maryland was erected in 1697; the second in 1704.

After the establishment of Baltimore, its splendid harbor facilities soon led to the development of considerable trade extending from the rich Chesapeake Bay country into coastwise activity. Trade with Philadelphia, New York, and Boston was followed by trade with London, Baltic and Mediterranean ports. After the Revolution there was developed that unique sailing ship of commerce, the Baltimore clipper, called a "clipper" some twenty-five years before the so-called clipper-ship era. These fast ships brought the riches of the Orient and

118

the Mediterranean to Baltimore in trade. In their cargoes were fine English furniture and fine furniture from France and Italy. It is likely that some furniture from Portugal and Spain came to Baltimore.

One thing is quite sure. Baltimore, after the Revolution, was one of the most prolific sources of beautifully styled furniture. The cabinetwork combined many elements of the Directoire and the Sheraton styles in a way that was unique with Baltimore and whose counterpart was not created by either the masters of Salem, by Phyfe of New York, or by Connelly of Philadelphia.

One of the characteristics of Baltimore Hepplewhite furniture is inlaid plaques of glass painted in gold, on a black background, depicting classical figures. This feature appears in the form of inlaid ovals and cartouches. Many roll-top desks, with rolling section either in one piece of barrel-like design or in the form of a tambour, are known to have been made not only for Baltimore buyers but also for the wealthy planters of Virginia and Maryland.

No less than three hundred cabinetmakers were working in Maryland between 1750 and 1820. Among these were Italians, Dutchmen, Frenchmen, and Irishmen, most of whom worked in Baltimore. The cabinetmakers at Annapolis seem to have been Englishmen and they used cherry as a substitute for walnut and mahogany before the Revolution. John Shaw was perhaps the most famous eighteenth-century cabinetmaker of Annapolis. Isaac Johns explained, in the Maryland *Journal,* that while he could not boast a European education he had certain apprentices such as William Moore, an excellent cabinetmaker, and that he was prepared to do good work. From 1750 many Baltimore and Annapolis merchants advertised household furniture of the very best kind, including tables, elbow chairs, sideboards, looking glasses, and other items. As early as 1740 ships were entering the Chesapeake with furniture as ballast. In 1768 Charles Carroll of Maryland, damning the Stamp Act and the Townsend Act, politely informed an English correspondent that American craftsmen were ready to produce all of the things which theretofore had been imported from England.

Baltimore, Annapolis, and other Maryland cities enjoyed a considerable production of fancy chairs. Some of the fancy chairs made at Baltimore are among the finest known. There are sets of painted chairs on the back panels of which are scenes depicted as meticulously and as realistically as landscapes—and they are actual scenes of homes, estates, and plantations of Maryland. Up to now only one book, *Baltimore Furniture, 1760–1810*, has done justice to the Baltimore-Annapolis area as one of America's important style centers. Few people realize that Baltimore was, literally, the supply depot for much of the furniture and many of the elegancies that went into Washington and Georgetown after it was decided to place the nation's capital city on the Potomac. Some Baltimore cabinetmakers moved southward into Georgetown and Alexandria, Virginia, and, incidentally, some cabinetmakers from Alexandria moved into Baltimore. Baltimore's influence was almost entirely to the southward. If you look at its position on the Chesapeake Bay, it is readily noted that Baltimore had water access to all of the Tidewater plantation country of Virginia and Carolina and could deliver to private docks everything that was ordered by the wealthy planters of the South. Because of the advantages of the Chesapeake, Baltimore could do business far more expeditiously with Charleston and Savannah than could New York or Philadelphia.

Chapter X

PENNSYLVANIA

IT WAS not until the late 1920s that collectors of Pennsylvania pioneer furniture began to realize that many of Pennsylvania's pioneer furniture patterns derive from Sweden. In the roaring, prohibitive, and exhibitive 1920s, when prices of American antiques reached an all-time high and when fine pioneer furniture was bringing fantastic prices, several shiploads of Swedish antiques were brought over and unloaded at Boston and Baltimore. Much of this furniture filtered into Pennsylvania and found ready sale as genuine Pennsylvania antiques. This Swedish provincial furniture was almost identical with early Pennsylvania furniture because it was cut from the same patterns and much of it was fashioned from the same kind of wood—pine.

Swedish-type furniture, introduced about 1640, and made on the spot by Swedish artisans up to 1750, did not, however, reign alone in the Delaware Valley. By 1650 the Dutch were on the scene, claiming both sides of the Delaware River. They brought to the land that is now Pennsylvania substantially the same furniture traditions that obtained in their great colony of New Amsterdam. Swedish and Dutch furniture of pioneer type is not dissimilar, partly because the Netherlands had quite an extensive trade with her Scandinavian neighbor. The Swedes, however, were not so well acquainted with the furniture styles of China as were the Dutch, whose mer-

PENNSYLVANIA

TRUMPET-FOOT HIGHBOY WITH SECRET DRAWER
MOLDING AT TOP

BROKEN-ARCH HIGHBOY WITH FRAME
FINIALS AND TYPICAL SAVERY
DECORATION

chants were constantly trading with the Chinese and with the East Indies. The Dutch kas and other heavy Dutch household furniture of the first half of the seventeenth century were in Pennsylvania, or more properly New Sweden, long before William Penn arrived. The Dutch style known as William and Mary was in Pennsylvania before the William and Mary style became popular in England when these monarchs were invited over from the Netherlands to reign over Great Britain in place of the deposed King James II.

When William Penn arrived, he brought with him, as surviving letters indicate, considerable furniture of the high styles of the court of Charles II. But certain of his letters, which preceded his arrival, also ordered furniture made in advance of his coming, indicating he knew that cabinetmakers were on the spot.

With the arrival of Penn and the establishment of his religious-freedom colony, his land was opened up to the oppressed as well as to the adventurous of England, Scotland, Ireland, Wales, the Netherlands, France, Switzerland, and the Palatinate. The Swedes and the Dutch who were there long before him readily accepted his benign rule. They were glad also to resolve their own differences, which were nothing more than an echo of the national differences between the Netherlands and Sweden in respect of their bids for power in Europe and the New World. The Dutch and the Swedes became solid and substantial citizens of Penn's new colony.

Swiss pioneer furniture, especially in the form of all-wood chairs similar to the *sgabello* of Italy, hanging cupboards, and stretcher tables with hutches under tilting tops, were once quite common in the valleys of Pennsylvania settled by the Mennonites. The room designated as Pennsylvania-German in the American Wing of the Metropolitan Museum displays a Swiss-type side table,

TURNED MEDIAL STRETCHER TABLE

TEA TABLE WITH SHELL CARVING AND
ACANTHUS DECORATION

a Swedish-type sawbuck table, a Swedish-type chest, a Dutch hanging cupboard, a Swedish armchair, and an early Georgian paneled mantel with a scene-painted panel. This room is typical of an early Pennsylvania farmhouse, but it is not, by any stretch of the imagination, a Pennsylvania-German room. It is a Pennsylvania room, echoing out of the past of at least four different countries. Swiss-style pioneer furniture did not persist so long in Pennsylvania as did the Dutch and Swedish types which were, perhaps, better adapted to the demands of life on a Pennsylvania farm. However, the Swiss and Swedish tradition of painted decoration on furniture and on chests persisted well into the nineteenth century.

It has been said by certain commentators that only rude caves and huts marked the site of Philadelphia when Penn arrived. This is not true. The house of Gunnar Rambo, built in 1662, was then standing, as were many other houses of brick, stone, and log construction, built not only by the Swedes but also by the Dutch. Up to 1840 and even later Swedish and Dutch houses were still standing in the City of Brotherly Love.

The furniture used by the original Dutch and Swedish settlers of Pennsylvania became the prototype of practically all of the pioneer furniture of Pennsylvania down to 1850. Calling it Pennsylvania German because it was the favorite furniture of thousands of German immigrants or because they made furniture in imitation of it, or because they used it second or third hand, does not alter its ancestry and its provenance.

Almost every county or shire of England was represented in the first shiploads of Englishmen to come to Penn's colony. The good town of Philadelphia became America's first boom town, growing faster even than its proprietor had ever imagined a town could grow. Penn's colony was prosperous from the very beginning. His

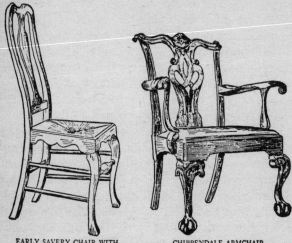

EARLY SAVERY CHAIR WITH
SCROLLED SKIRT

CHIPPENDALE ARMCHAIR

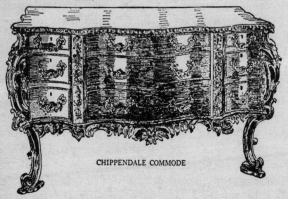

CHIPPENDALE COMMODE

liberality provided for the entry of hundreds and thousands of European artisans and workmen, certain of whom indentured themselves as servants for a period of years to any who would pay their passage money. When indentured to cabinetmakers, silversmiths, or potters they learned to work in the styles favored by their masters who were either English, or of Dutch or Swedish ancestry.

The soil of Penn's three original counties, Buckingham, Chester, and Philadelphia, as well as the fourth county, Lancaster, paid such rich rewards in crops that food was ever abundant. Children and grandchildren of original Swedish settlers moved up the Schuylkill Valley into land that was later made into the fifth county of Pennsylvania, Berks.

With Philadelphia multiplying its number of dwellings year after year, there was a tremendous demand for furniture. Consequently, furniture production in Penn's city started on a considerable scale not later than 1685. This town, destined to be the most important eighteenth-century city in the colonies, became a port of entry for additional thousands of French, Flemish, Dutch, Swiss, and German immigrants, many of whom were desirous of settling in the Township of Conestoken, or Conestoga, which the Swiss came to call New Switzerland, the French Heavenly Lorraine, and which the Flemish considered the equivalent of their own homeland. With these entrants came many Welsh people who, having settled west of Philadelphia in a manor given them by Penn, discovered that deposits of iron existed in Conestoken together with great stands of timber for making charcoal. Some Cornish settlers made the same discovery. The Conestoga Valley became the nucleus of a new county and county seat. Thus Philadelphia had an extension of itself in the new town of Lancaster.

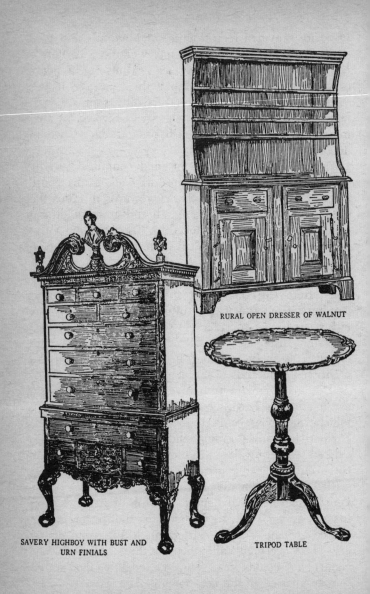

RURAL OPEN DRESSER OF WALNUT

SAVERY HIGHBOY WITH BUST AND
URN FINIALS

TRIPOD TABLE

By the time Lancaster was established as a town in 1730, the joiners and turners of Philadelphia had developed a new type of pioneer chair of all-wood construction. It was sturdy. It would take lots of punishment. Yet it was so utterly delightful in shape and form that it was purchased by the wealthy. This was the "Philadelphia chair" which, on sight, captured the interest of all who saw it. Today it is called the American Windsor chair. It is Pennsylvania's first great contribution to a national chair style. Eventually this type of chair was made in every one of the colonies. Many colonial chairmakers invented delightful variants of the original Philadelphia chair.

Following the inventors of the Philadelphia chair came a group of cabinetmakers, highly skilled, plying their trade within the most liberal of all colonial governments and having custom that was growing richer and richer year by year. This group of Philadelphia cabinetmakers began making fine walnut and mahogany furniture in the style of Queen Anne, and with the refinements of Queen Anne which today we designate as Georgian. This furniture is often called Philadelphia Chippendale because it incorporates certain of the designs made popular by Chippendale. But the vast proportion of this Philadelphia furniture displays the cabriole leg with carved knees and with ball-and-claw feet—the latter an element not found in any of Chippendale's designs with the single exception of a bedpost foot which, significantly, does not appear in all copies of his published work. Some of this Philadelphia School furniture, notably the masterpieces by Benjamin Randolph, features the cabriole leg and French "turned-up" foot which Chippendale borrowed from the styles of Louis XV. Randolph's work is as fine and as ornate as the most elaborate work of London's royal cabinetmakers.

CHIPPENDALE
SERPENTINE-FRONT CHEST OF DRAWERS WITH
DWARFED CABRIOLE LEGS

RURAL PAINTED PINE DOWER CHEST

By 1740 the prosperity enjoyed by Philadelphia was general throughout the entire Pennsylvania colony. English cabinetmakers found in Philadelphia a far more lucrative and consistent custom than they could find in London. They came to Philadelphia and, noting the entire absence of adherence to traditional design in the work of established cabinetmakers, soon began the production of original work of their own.

Plunket Fleeson in 1742 offered several sorts of good chair frames with black and red leather covering, finished cheaper than any made in Philadelphia or imported from Boston. Evidently Philadelphia could not produce all the furniture it required, so it was buying furniture from Boston. As early as 1729 red leather was noted in the *American Weekly Mercury* of Philadelphia as being used startlingly to upholster the seats and backs of chairs. This was close to twenty-five years before Mr. Chippendale advocated the use of red leather as an upholstery material!

The early-eighteenth century cabinetmakers of Philadelphia were so busy that they supported manufactories which specialized in the making of parts for furniture, which the cabinetmakers purchased ready for use. These manufacturers of furniture parts made columns for tables, legs for chairs, and other elements which could be assembled quickly in the shops of the cabinetmakers.

Furniture production in Philadelphia on this grand scale developed great craftsmen such as Savery, Randolph, and Gostelow. Savery was a Quaker, born in 1722. He became a property owner in his late teens. At the age of twenty-four he had an income of £52 a year from real estate he owned. He entered Philadelphia politics and yet was so industrious at his trade that he became one of the finest cabinetmakers of the New World. His early furniture was in the simpler styles of

CHINESE CHIPPENDALE

CARVED FLEMISH CHAIR WITH
LEATHER BACK

CHIPPENDALE CHAIR SHOWING ROCOCO
INFLUENCE

the Queen Anne period. Savery apparently began as a chairmaker. His first label locates him "at a sign of the chair near the market on Second Street." After 1762 Savery's work was obviously influenced by Chippendale's *Cabinetmakers' Director*. He was probably the first American cabinetmaker to borrow from Chippendale. Yet even Savery's finest pieces sometimes display the claw-and-ball foot, which is essentially Georgian and not Chippendale. Savery apparently started what is today called the Philadelphia School of Cabinetmaking. We may be quite sure that he was wholly unconscious of starting anything other than the making of fine furniture which many cabinetmakers envied and which other cabinetmakers equaled. Randolph, John Elliott, Jr., and Jonathan Gostelow, the grandson of a Swedish settler, did equally good work even though they are not quite so famous as Savery. Claypool, Affleck, Clifton, Folwell, Joseph and Stephen Armit, and William Wayne were Philadelphia cabinetmakers who followed in the footsteps of the master, William Savery. Later Connelly was making furniture as fine as any made by Duncan Phyfe.

On June 20, 1775, John Folwell, cabinetmaker and furniture designer of Front Street, and John Norman, engraver, in Second Street, Philadelphia, issued a most interesting broadside. They proposed jointly to publish, at fifty shillings a copy, what would have been the great *Philadelphia Cabinetmakers' Design Book*. Within little more than a year the Revolution had started and the enterprise was abandoned. That is why the proposed American *Gentlemen's and Cabinetmakers' Assistant*, with two hundred ingenious designs by Folwell, engraved by Norman on sixty folio size copper plates, was not printed. But printed firmly in the minds of all Philadelphia cabinetmakers was the style that had developed in the Quaker City—a style always as good as the prevailing fashion of London and Paris, and often showing an advance in cabinetmaking execution over the work of the general craftsmen of these two European capitals.

In Lancaster County, in the Welsh village of Lampeter, a Swiss-trained cabinetmaker named John Bachman was, after 1765, making furniture that on more than one occasion has been attributed to the Philadelphia School. Bachman made fine furniture and clock cases. His furniture, very much in the style of Louis XV, was sold largely to Lancaster County people of wealth and refinement. Bachman's clock cases were sold to clockmakers who, by 1765, flourished in and around Lancaster in great numbers. They made tall clocks. These were expensive clocks. Yet Lancaster town and county absorbed all that a half score or more clockmakers produced.

Michael Lund, a Swedish cabinetmaker of Lancaster, was producing walnut furniture in Queen Anne and Georgian styles as late as 1755. In Lancaster also were Windsor chairmakers and producers of pioneer-type furniture used by the farmers in the Conestoga Valley.

Immediately to the west a huge new township of Lancaster County was in process of settlement. In 1749 this finally became York County. It was originally peopled by Marylanders who moved northward across the poorly defined boundary between Calvert's colony and Penn's, and by settlers from Lancaster County. The town of York was founded in 1741 and shortly thereafter cabinetmakers and chairmakers were at work. In 1830 there were ten cabinetmakers and five chairmakers in the little town of York, supplying the needs of less than five thousand people. In Pennsylvania, founding a new town meant not only the immediate establishment of artisans' shops to supply that town, but also sufficient shops to supply the surrounding county until other new towns were formed.

GATE-LEG TABLE WITH SPANISH FEET

CHIPPENDALE PIER TABLE

Reading, established in 1752, as the county seat of Berks County, had its chairmakers, cabinetmakers, and clockmakers by 1755. There was a silversmith at work in Lancaster by 1740. Philadelphia enjoyed silversmiths and pewterers before the year 1700 dawned. With the beginning of the nineteenth century there were so many cabinetmakers at work in Pennsylvania, so many silversmiths, pewterers, clockmakers, chairmakers, and others, that the production was enormous. It had to be. Pennsylvania, the keystone of the colonies, became the keystone commonwealth of the federal Union. After New York held the honor for a short period, Philadelphia became the capital city of the Union until the city of Washington was laid out and built.

Chief among the now popular antiques of Pennsylvania are its plain pine, plain walnut, and its painted and decorated pioneer-type furniture which, often designated as Pennsylvania-German, is actually of Swiss, Dutch, and Swedish origin. Swedish and Finnish chests made as early as 1680 in southern New Jersey display almost precisely the same characteristics as chests made in Pennsylvania between 1750 and 1850. Chests made in the Conestoga Valley in Pennsylvania have architectural fronts with arched panels. Most of the chests made elsewhere have the panels painted on. Not all of these chests have painted decoration. Some few are beautifully formed of fine cabinet woods such as walnut and mahogany. Some are made of cherry.

In 1825 every town of any consequence in Pennsylvania, and this includes Easton, Bethlehem, Reading, York, Harrisburg, and Pittsburgh, as well as Philadelphia and Lancaster, had anywhere from one to a half-dozen fancy chairmakers, producing chairs very similar to those now designated as Hitchcock type. It is all very well for us to use the term Hitchcock in designating the

BIRD-CAGE TILT-TOP TABLE
WITH PIE-CRUST TOP

SAVERY PIER TABLE WITH MARBLE TOP

American fancy chair, but by 1836 there were at least two chair factories in Pittsburgh that produced fancy chairs at a rate which equaled Hitchcock's production. These factories made chairs not only for local use, but for the Ohio River trade. They also specialized in fitting out river steamboat salons and staterooms with fancy chairs.

Pennsylvania was fortunate in having many good architects. Most of these, now unhonored, unsung, and unknown, designed magnificent Georgian houses which in turn influenced furniture design. The fine Georgian house was not peculiar to Philadelphia. We find Georgian styling in the mansions of the iron masters still standing in the Conestoga and Schuylkill Valleys. Pennsylvania is rich in Georgian churches and spires, some of the early ones redolent of the designs of Sir Christopher Wren.

Philadelphia was a center of art and culture from 1725. Philadelphia enjoyed what might well be termed mass production of fine furniture, mirrors, and other elegancies from 1750. Wherever there was a settlement, a village, or a town, there collectible antiques were produced as new merchandise for the people. Pennsylvania's people enjoyed the fertility of the soil, the riches of the mines, and the freedom of mind and opportunity that William Penn insisted would be the keystone of his charter. Pennsylvanians were lucky. Penn's philosophy of government included making peace with the Indians before settlement was attempted. Consequently the colony of Pennsylvania had less Indian troubles and more friendly relations than did any other of the original colonies.

Other items of antiquarian interest which should be mentioned here are Pennsylvania ironwork and Pennsylvania pen work. The ironwork falls into two cate-

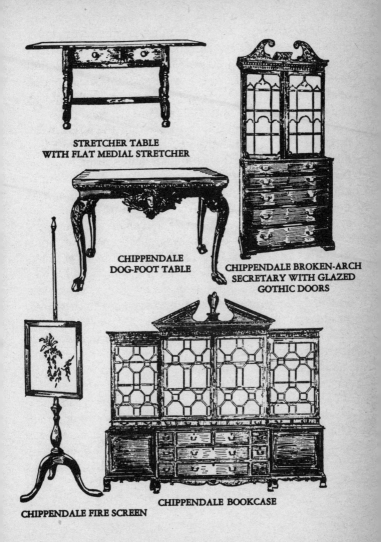

STRETCHER TABLE
WITH FLAT MEDIAL STRETCHER

CHIPPENDALE
DOG-FOOT TABLE

CHIPPENDALE BROKEN-ARCH
SECRETARY WITH GLAZED
GOTHIC DOORS

CHIPPENDALE FIRE SCREEN

CHIPPENDALE BOOKCASE

gories: wrought iron and cast iron. Of all the colonies
Pennsylvania was the largest eighteenth-century producer of iron. Great quantities of ornamental wrought
iron in the form of hinges, hasps, et cetera, were produced. Produced also were thousands of stove plates,
cast with beautiful low-relief decoration, with biblical
and with stylized floral motifs. Pennsylvania penwork,
often called *Fraktur*, is a form of what the French call
imagèrie populaire. The motifs displayed—hearts, tulips,
birds, and geometric forms—derive largely from Swedish,
Dutch, French, Swiss, and Irish designs. The latter are
impressed, perhaps by remote control, from the Irish
Book of Kells. Many pieces of Pennsylvania *Fraktur* are
in the form of house blessings or memorials. Some few
are historic. One maker of these, Gabriel Miesse, flourished between 1835 and 1850. He was born of Swiss
parentage in Bern township, Berks County. At least 90
per cent of the *Fraktur* was made by, or for, Palatinates
and their progeny. Some examples were made by school-
teachers.

One other item, commonly called chalkware, is often
attributed to Pennsylvania. It is actually the cheapest
"boughten" type of ornament ever made for the people:
plaster casts, daubed with touches of color, in imitation
of Staffordshire figures. Such figures were made and
vended from barrows, carts, and trays by street and road
peddlers in many cities and towns in all the states from
about 1800 down to 1860. There is nothing distinctly
"Pennsylvania" about them. Most of this chalkware was
made by Italians.

**WINDSOR CHAIR
WITH BAMBOO TURNING**

**Brace-Bow-back
1725-1750**

**Hoop-back with Comb
1725-1750**

**Comb-back, arm
1730-1750**

**High bow-back, arm
1730-1760**

**Writing-Arm, Roundabout
1750-1800**

Eight-Legged Settee 1750-1775

**Fan-back
1750-1775**

CHILD'S WINDSOR CHAIR

WINDSOR TABLE

**TRIPOD CANDLE-
STAND WITH
SCREW TOP**

HEAVY ROUNDABOUT WINDSOR CHAIR

Chapter XI

DELAWARE

First settled by the Dutch at Zwaanendael in 1631, and then by Swedes in 1638, what is now Delaware was once a part of Penn's grant known as the three lower counties. These three counties finally achieved partition and separate colonial status. Delaware was one of the thirteen original states. The three counties of this state are rich in surviving old structures, relics of Dutch, Swedish, and English settlement and occupation. The early furniture styles of Delaware are, almost without exception, the same as those of Pennsylvania. The same pioneer furniture, the same William and Mary, Queen Anne, and Georgian furniture that graced the homes of Philadelphia and Lancaster were in Wilmington and other Delaware towns.

There was considerable fancy-chair production in Delaware after 1813. It is fairly evident that Windsor or Philadelphia chairs were made in Wilmington by 1750. There were potteries in operation and rich deposits of kaolin clay were tapped in the eighteenth century. America's first porcelain works at Philadelphia used Delaware clays.

The duPont family settled on the banks of the Brandywine early in the federal era and there established the powder and chemical industry that has become an international organization. Paper mills have dotted the Brandywine Valley since colonial days. Most of the citizens of Delaware have always been well-to-do. Perhaps more fine furniture was owned here per capita between 1750 and 1850 than in any other region of the country. Silversmiths were at work early in the history of Wilmington. *Silversmiths of Delaware 1700–1850* by Jessie Harrington is required reading for all students and collectors interested in the precious metal wares made by the artisans of this state. Perhaps the finest collection of American antiques now extant is today in Delaware —the Henry du Pont collection housed at the Winterthur estate. Mr. du Pont has recently opened this collection to public view on certain days, by appointment.

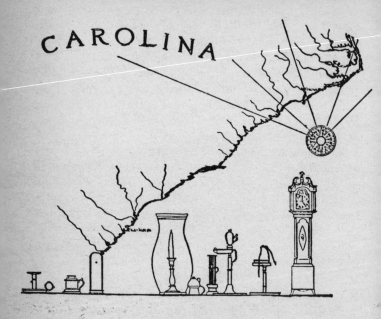

CAROLINA

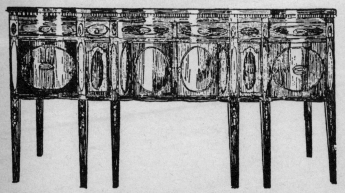

HEPPLEWHITE SIDEBOARD

Chapter XII

THE CAROLINAS

IN 1663 the great liberal philosopher John Locke, together with Anthony Ashley Cooper, Lord Shaftesbury, Lord Clarendon, and others, was granted a tract of land in America called the Province of Carolina which, with extensions thereof granted by Charles II who succeeded Cromwell, included what is now North and South Carolina, north Georgia, and everything to the west—theoretically to the Pacific. This land was granted to erect a "democracy" under a new form of fundamental constitution designed to make it a utopia. The population—that is, the people—were to be hereditary "leetmen" or servants of the soil. Above them was an upper middle class called lords of the manor, who were permitted to let out tenant farms of small acreage. Over both these classes was to be a self-perpetuating colonial noblesse, having powers comparable to petty princes. Crowning the entire political fabric were the proprietors—the boys who owned the whole works. The oldest of these was to be the viceroy, the next the admiral, next the chamberlain, then the high chief justice, the chancellor, and the treasurer.

The entire province was to be divided into squares, or counties, each county into signories, then into baronies and then into precincts. It was about the weirdest and most impractical political setup for a colony ever imagined. Needless to say, it did not work. But it did start the settlement of Carolina.

An attempt to maintain the type of government

originally conceived led to several internal colonial revolts which by 1707 resulted in the establishment of one royal governor over the Carolinas, with a lieutenant governor located at Charleston and another at Albemarle. In 1710 Governor Hyde, a cousin of Queen Anne, was made the first governor of North Carolina as a separate colony. A more stable and liberal government then obtained in both North and South Carolina. Charleston, the chief city of South Carolina, became one of the centers of Southern culture and refinement.

As early as 1666 the lord proprietors of the Carolina colony invited artisans to emigrate to America. By the last quarter of the sevententh century cabinetmakers were at work. But there is no record to tell in what style they worked or for whom. However, in light of the unique political philosophy that obtained, we may assume that crude furniture was made for the lowly serfs and that some fairly good furniture was either imported or made on the spot for the ruling classes.

By 1732 Charleston had a newspaper and in that newspaper cabinetmakers advertised for bespoke work, meaning they were ready to take orders for furniture to be made. There were chairmakers and cabinetmakers and other artists and artisans from London working in Charleston from 1732 onward. A tabulated record of all cabinetmakers at work between 1732 and the Revolution, as mentioned in newspapers and other documents, leads to the conclusion that close to a hundred practitioners of the furniture-making craft were at work. Consequently Charleston and Carolina furniture in general may be said to begin with the Georgian style and that always the Georgian and the succeeding styles of Chippendale, Adam, Hepplewhite, the Directoire, and Sheraton were made in the best manner for the Carolina gentry. The plantation owners of Carolina were just as

meticulous in their demands as were the plantation owners of Virginia. It must also be admitted that considerable furniture entered the port of Charleston from
Boston, New York, and Philadelphia. The first of the
customers of Lambert Hitchcock's chair-parts factory in
Connecticut were the chairmakers of Charleston. These
men were actually making, for sale in Carolina, the
chairs today called Hitchcock before Hitchcock himself
went into the chair-manufacturing business.

After 1800 Charleston enjoyed a general production of
excellent furniture in the Directoire and Sheraton styles.
Much of this furniture was comparable to that produced
by Duncan Phyfe in New York. The swing to Empire,
however, seems to have hit Charleston and the Carolinas
before it made much of an impression northward, and at
least ten years before it achieved any popularity in
Baltimore and New York. This may have been because
of the considerable French complexion of a part of Carolina's population and to the *émigrés* who rejoiced at the
end of the Directoire and the re-establishment of the
French Empire, even though under Napoleon. Almost
all Carolina furniture made after 1825 is Empire-heavy,
unimaginative, ornate, and important only in respect of
its size, its bulk, and its expanse of highly varnished
veneered woods.

The silversmiths of Charleston and other Carolina
towns made much fine silver that is today considered
on a parity with the production of any of our silversmiths of the 1750-1850 century. Much Carolina silver
was stolen by renegade slaves and thieving Union sol-
diers during the war between the states. Carpetbagging
politicians also took their share of this valuable metal
ware. These thieves probably sold their loot at the price
of the precious metal. But a goodly portion of this fine
Southern silver was secreted and did not fall to looters.

EMPIRE BED WITH PINEAPPLE POST

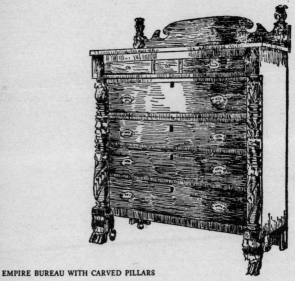

EMPIRE BUREAU WITH CARVED PILLARS

CHARACTERISTIC
EARLY EMPIRE CHAIR

EARLY EMPIRE CARVED CONSOLE TABLE
WITH CARVED PEDESTAL

Many impoverished families of Carolina were later forced to sell their precious old furniture and silver. Perhaps two thirds of Carolina's finest antiques have been destroyed or dissipated. What remains in the hands of descendants of the original owners does, however, indicate that fine furniture and silver were made in the Carolinas and in quantity sufficient to supply the demands of a meticulous population of planters, merchants, and professional men.

SHERATON CARD TABLE

SHERATON SIDEBOARD

SHERATON SECRETARY

Chapter XIII

GEORGIA

THE colony of Georgia was founded by a number of benevolent and socially conscious gentlemen of London. They planned to establish a refuge for the poor and for those who, by misfortune of debt, had been placed in the sponging houses, workhouses, and jails of England. They also had their eyes on persecuted sects of Continental Europe who might conceivably be coaxed to the new colony in mass emigrations. Politically, the advisors to George II were interested in the scheme for military reasons. They wanted a strong colony in the South to serve as a barrier against possible advances of the Spanish upward from Florida and the Gulf coast.

Oglethorpe, an experienced general and a man of great liberality, was selected by the London trustees as first governor. In 1733 they founded the city of Savannah and established the colony of Georgia. They were, perhaps, unaware of the fact that in founding Savannah as the chief city of their colony of salvation for the oppressed they were also founding a city that within half a century was to become a competitor of aristocratic Charleston.

Georgia became another colony of plantations. The pattern for settlement established by the aristocrats in Virginia and settlers in the Carolinas was followed by the former "crackers" out of the British prisons. These people, not malefactors, criminals, or jail-birds were

designated as "crackers" because they "cracked jail" or
escaped from debtors' imprisonment upon promise to
emigrate. Freed of their liabilities, they established an
aristocracy of their own, marked by tolerance, under-
standing, and a great neighborliness, or homeliness.

Very early in Georgia's history we find cabinetmaking
being done by itinerants who would move from one
settlement or plantation to another, making what was
needed from local wood as best they could make it
to fulfill the needs of the inhabitants. It is recorded
that cabinetmaking was taught by itinerants to Negro
slaves who apparently enjoyed greater freedom in Georgia than in any other Southern colony. There is also
record of a Welsh cabinetmaker named Jermyn Davis
who worked as an itinerant producer of really fine furniture for Georgia estates between 1770 and 1820. There
are documentary records still extant to bolster the legends regarding the travels of this man through Georgia.
From these it would appear that he worked on some
plantations as a supervising cabinetmaker and designer
for other workers, some of whom were slaves. It is now
believed that Jermyn Davis entered Georgia from the
Welsh barony of Pennsylvania, established by William
Penn about 1685, and settled by many members of the
Davis or Davies family.

Georgia was not a producer of furniture in sufficient
quantities even for its own needs and, consequently, the
antiques of Georgia cannot be classified entirely as made
on the land. Imports of furniture from Baltimore, Boston,
Philadelphia, and New York are recorded from between
1750 and 1860. At Savannah, Hitchcock chairs were
made from parts produced by Lambert Hitchcock in his
Connecticut factory before Hitchcock himself produced
complete chairs. Tremendous quantities of heavy Empire
and early Victorian furniture poured into Georgia during

its early boom years, 1820-60. Some furniture of the same type was made at Savannah and at Atlanta. This is the *Gone-with-the-Wind* furniture that everybody knows about today because of the motion picture dramatization of Margaret Mitchell's novel. It is significant that in *Gone with the Wind* the Irishman O'Hara becomes a plantation owner. This is entirely in character with the settlement and development of Georgia. The state, as well as the colony, offered a refuge to the unfortunates and to all who had failed to develop their full potentialities elsewhere. The colony was a Southern one. Its traditions, in so far as development and settlement were concerned, were entirely Southern. Yet the attitude of mind and the philosophy of life of the typical Georgian were that of a Pennsylvanian or New Englander. They were that kind of people.

Many fancy chairs found in Georgia and in northern Florida were, as we have noted, apparently made by Savannah cabinetmakers and sold to all and sundry. Sets of fancy chairs are frequently found in Georgia as well as in South Carolina and northern Florida. Some of these chairs were assembled from parts made in Connecticut.

English-made Regency and Empire furniture is also found in Georgia. The colonization of Georgia did not end with its being made a state. There was a continuous influx of English people who, having achieved sufficient funds to purchase cheap lands, entered Georgia with enough furniture to furnish a home, enough money to buy the land, build a home, and start business as a plantation owner or a cotton grower.

Chapter XIV

OHIO

No GEOGRAPHY of American antiques can be complete without inclusion of Ohio which, admitted to the Union in 1802, became a production center for its own population and finally for the people of at least ten other states. Marietta, Cincinnati, and Chillicothe were the chief southern settlements of Ohio. Along the northern lake shore, then considered a part of Connecticut's Western Reserve, people from Connecticut and New York State established settlements. Shortly after 1785 the territory that was to become Ohio became a melting pot that included people from Pennsylvania, western Virginia, New York, and New England. That is why almost every type and kind of so-called Pennsylvania folk art is found in Ohio. That is why fancy chairs and Windsor chairs displaying variations considered peculiar to Connecticut, New York, Massachusetts, and Pennsylvania are found throughout Ohio.

But something else of considerable antiquarian importance happened in this new state. It was the first state to be built under the Greek revival influence. Ohio is still rich in Greek revival architecture in its every manifestation. The state also became a center of manufacture for classic revival furniture. Geographically Ohio was destined to become a great production center for many other territories and new states as the path of empire moved westward.

John Broadfoot Smith established a cabinetmaking shop in Cincinnati about 1815. So famed and well considered was this cabinetmaker in 1819 that he was selected to address the master mechanics of Cincinnati in celebration of the forty-third year of American independence. John Broadfoot Smith's cabinetmaking shop finally became a factory which employed sixty people by 1850. In that year it had a production of one thousand center tables, twelve hundred sofas, twenty-five hundred parlor chairs, and other items in proportion. It is, perhaps, likely that Smith's furniture factory was the first in Cincinnati. In 1830 it was, however, but one of many shops which, collectively, issued their own illustrated book of prices. This was the first cabinetmaker's price book printed west of Pittsburgh and was issued not six months after Joseph Snowden printed the first price book for the cabinetmakers of Pittsburgh.

The early Cincinnati price book shows furniture-style elements of almost exactly the patterns made famous by Duncan Phyfe, a blending of Directoire with the best styling of Sheraton. In 1836 the United Society of Journeymen Cabinetmakers of Cincinnati issued another price book with illustrations. This book pictures many new elements and a considerable coarsening of the older elements of design as used by the cabinetmakers of 1830. Which is to say that the designs shown in the 1836 Cincinnati price book are almost wholly in the Empire style.

By 1836 Cincinnati was one of the largest furniture-manufacturing centers in America. Ten years later it was the largest furniture-manufacturing center in America. In 1840 more than three hundred people were employed at Cincinnati producing annually over half a million dollars' worth of furniture. In 1850 Cincinnati employed more than a thousand people in the production of well over one million five hundred thousand dollars' worth of furniture every year. Between 1830 and 1850 at least ten million dollars' worth of furniture was produced in Cincinnati.

Examples of the volume of furniture production can be gathered from individual records of the companies. For example, the Cincinnati Bureau Manufacturing Company produced seven thousand bureaus annually in addition to much other furniture. By 1850 the Blakeslee Mirror Factory was producing twenty-five hundred mirrors a week. Blakeslee's mirror production included tabernacle types with paintings on glass in the upper panels. This firm sold mirrors at wholesale to furniture and houseware dealers throughout the entire Ohio, Mississippi, and Missouri River systems. Burley and Lyford of Cincinnati had a factory for the mass production of cottage furniture and fancy chairs in the Italian and Greek styles. Their line included enameled, painted, scrolled, and landscape decorated beds, bureaus, chairs, and toilet stands. These were sold through furniture stores everywhere west of Cincinnati and used to furnish thousands of river steamboat cabins. From data thus far assembled Burley and Lyford seemed to have been established prior to 1836.

Henry Closterman's exclusive fancy-chair factory was in production at Cincinnati in 1845. Closterman is one of several dozen fancy-chair makers of Ohio whose chairs are today bought and sold as "Hitchcock type." Perhaps the most extensive chair manufactory of Cincinnati was the Coddington Works which, in 1850, boasted a production of one hundred and eighty thousand chairs a year. These were sold wholesale at from $4.25 to $22 a dozen. Coddington's output was largely fancy chairs, painted and gilded. The firm did business with furniture dealers in Texas, Louisiana, Arkansas,

Mississippi, Georgia, Kentucky, Indiana, and Illinois. Other Cincinnati chairmakers and cabinetmakers of note, and of considerable production, were E. B. Dobell, Dobell and Hughes, McAlpin, and John Geyer, who succeeded McAlpin. This factory in 1850 was a five-story establishment devoted to the production of Italian and fancy parlor chairs, sofas, marble-top tables, papier-mâché tables, and stands.

C. B. Johnston founded a chair factory at Cincinnati in 1842 which produced at least a half-million fancy chairs in its first decade of operation. Scarrett & Mason, furniture dealers of St. Louis, had a standing order with Johnston for thirty-five thousand fancy chairs per year. That kind of production puts the efforts of Mr. Hitchcock into the category of amateur. Cincinnati literally deluged the ever-expanding West with fancy chairs. Some of them were produced in the same year Mr. Hitchcock went into production at his own factory in Connecticut.

Shaw and Rettig were cabinetmakers of Cincinnati who made exquisite mahogany and walnut furniture. Some of their work made between 1838 and 1842 is at times attributed to Duncan Phyfe. But this firm continued in business until after 1860. After making the Directoire-inspired furniture we call Phyfe, Shaw and Rettig made furniture in the Louis XIV antique style that we now call Victorian. Shaw and Rettig also made French-, Italian-, and Grecian-style bedsteads and painted cottage furniture from 1840 to 1860.

When the brothers Adam in the 1760s began using ancient Greek decorative forms in the residences and the furniture they designed for the nobility and the wealthy of England, "Greek revival" was an exclusive style. Thomas Hope, a Dutchman who made England his home late in the eighteenth century, looked upon Greek

revival as a style that could—and should—be popularized. The first American acceptance of Greek revival
style came immediately after the Revolution. It is found
in the work of that talented amateur architect, Thomas
Jefferson, and the influence he wielded in the design of
certain of the buildings erected in the nation's new
capital.

Most of our architects accepted Greek revival style
with open arms. This acceptance was fairly general by
1800. But the application of Greek revival architecture
was, of course, limited to new construction. After the
first settlement of Ohio and its admission as a state Ohio
had to be built. Because Greek revival was the dominant
style at that time we find the style incorporated somehow, someway, in almost every Ohio structure, whether
of brick, stone, or wood. The *Historical Collections of
Ohio,* issued in 1849, is illustrated with hundreds of
woodcuts which depict Greek revival architecture in
public buildings and private dwellings and farmhouses;
in churches, barns, pigsties, and outhouses.

In concerning ourselves with what Cincinnati contributed in the way of furniture production, it should not
be imagined that every Ohio village and town did not
have its own cabinetmakers and other craftsmen. They
did. Rhea Mansfield Knittle has listed hundreds of
cabinetmakers at work in Ohio villages and towns
between 1800 and 1850. She also has tabulated silversmiths, gunsmiths, pewterers, and potters. Mrs. Knittle
has contributed much to the history of another mass-
produced item today avidly collected as an antique—
Ohio glass. Comment on this Ohio antique is reserved
for a later chapter of this book.

Chapter XV

LIGHTING

COLONIAL lighting fixtures reflect one of the most curious anomalies in social history, although the anomaly is not readily apparent because of the pioneer character of our first colonizations. At any rate, this is the amazing story in a nutshell: our colonists, rich and poor, carried with them substantially the same type of lamp that was used by the citizens of Athens, Carthage, and Rome. We call it a fat—or Betty—lamp. Somehow civilization gave almost no thought to improvement of lighting for some five thousand years and then, in the space of less than two hundred and fifty years, from about 1700 onward to the present, carried lighting to the advanced stage we enjoy today.

Betty lamps, rush lights, and candles constituted the sum total of lighting methods known down to the middle of the eighteenth century. Of these only the candle could be burned readily without some sort of fixture or device. The Betty lamp in its crudest form is an open boat-shaped vessel with a wick trough—a fat or oil-burning dish. It provided a poor light, glimmering but faintly, and emitting dense black, smelly smoke. In New England, and perhaps also in Virginia, slivers of pitch pine, called candlewood, were often used in preference to Betty lamps. Sticks of this wood, impregnated by nature with resinous sap, were burned in holders, if one could contrive them, or simply inserted in a chink in the stone or brickwork of a fireplace.

Rush lights, made of fat-soaked pith of the swamp rush, and sometimes of the elderberry bush, were made in candle lengths and held at an angle in a pincerlike device on a stand. This, perforce, had to be a metallic holder, at least in part. The first iron ore found and worked in the colonies was discovered at Saugus, Massachusetts, not far from Boston. This ore was bog iron and, according to the records, it was at once fashioned into rushlight holders, Betty lamps, candlesticks, and agricultural tools.

Up to now no serious attempt have been made to classify all the various Betty lamps, rushlight holders, and candlesticks used by our forefathers in the seventeenth century. We shall not attempt classification in this book. One of the authors has collected lighting fixtures and devices for well over twenty-five years. Another has collected pictures, documents, and illustrated catalogues of lighting fixtures for about the same length of time. Jointly and severally we can say we have no two items exactly alike! You could, if you cared to, collect two thousand early Betty lamps and still have no two alike. That's the way it is when items are made one at a time, without sufficient materials on hand to make two alike even if the maker wanted to do so. Of course by 1750 many candlesticks were made in pairs, in foursomes, and even in half dozens, all alike. Eighty years after that the tinsmiths and whitesmiths were making simple candlesticks and lanterns on a mass-production basis. Also, any pewter wares used in lighting were apt to show close similarities because they were shaped with the standard fashioning patterns and cast in the same molds. But wrought-iron lighting fixtures and all-wood lighting standards of both the seventeenth and

EARLY RAILROAD
LANTERN

BLOWN-GLASS LANTERN

AN EARLY TIN LANTERN WITH
COW'S HORN WINDOW AND
DORMER DRAUGHTS

WATCHMAN'S LANTERN

Early lighting fixtures. Top left, side-wick lard-oil lamp; right, a portable lamp; lower left, adaptation of Dutch Stork lamp with a "pick-wick" in holder at side; lower right, two-wick portable lard-oil lamp.

eighteenth centuries were produced as individual items and apparently never as identical twins.

The actual construction of the small Betty lamp changed little through the years. The bodies were made of cast or wrought iron in one solid piece with a projecting spout in which the wick was placed. At the opposite end a curved handle was added. A short pick used in loosening the wick when it became embedded in grime was attached by a chain to this handle. In some of the Betty lamps a hooked spindle was also attached to this chain and used to hang the lamp on a convenient peg or chair back. In some sections of the country the lamp became an integral part of a stand that could be adjusted to various heights, and still others were set into holders fashioned to receive them. In time the vessels of these lamps became larger and we find some double Bettys hanging from a common staple. Although sheet iron was commonly used in making them, a few exist that were made of pottery. In general, the shape of all Bettys was elliptical, with one end drawn out to form the spout into which the wick was laid. The early examples usually have no covers, but in the later ones a flat piece of metal, pronged at the front to pass around the wick, was attached to a pivot at the back and slid sideways across the vessel. The lids on tin lamps were hinged and raised off the reservoir instead of sliding. Iron Bettys were superseded by lamps of tin and pewter.

A remarkable device for economy appeared in some of the lamps. A small gutter ran beneath the wick spout proper and as the drippings ran over the spout they were caught by the under gutter and carried into the vessel to be used again. As the wick was apt to draw more oil that could be consumed, this feature eliminated waste and protected the floor from the oily drippings.

Making rushlights was a household task, tedious and

EARLY PATENT LAMPS

dull. First the rushes had to be peeled of all outer covering save a narrow spine. This spine held the pith together and gave the section sufficient firmness for handling, drying, soaking in fat, and insertion in the holder. It is said that animal fats, fish oils, beeswax, and bayberry wax were all used in making rushlights. The holder for the rushlight had a metal clamp or pincerlike element to hold the rush. Otherwise the base, upright, and arm might be fashioned of any available wood. As we have stated, rushlight holders in infinite variety have been preserved. It is doubtful whether the Dutch in what is now New York and Pennsylvania used rushlights. Most of the holders here considered are of New England ancestry.

Candlemaking was also a general household task. The common people made their own candles; the servants of the rich and ruling classes did the work in the big houses and on the plantations and estates. Sheep suet and ox tallow were the major animal fats used in candles. Bayberry was the one vegetable fat used. The wax of the honeycomb was used when it could be had.

Making candles required cutting the fats into blocks, simmering in water, skimming, refining, and finally straining through a fine sieve, preferably of horsehair. Then came the forming which, in its crudest form, was hand moulding the warm wax, in gobs, around a wick of tow or cotton. The next and simpler method of making candles, and especially making in quantities, was by dipping. A great kettle of hot wax was made ready. Then prepared wicks, stiffened with wax, were lowered into the wax and immediately withdrawn. Upon cooling, they were again dipped, and so on, until sufficient coatings of hardening wax had been built up to the required candle diameter. Finally came the candle-molding process. A candle mold could be made of tinplate,

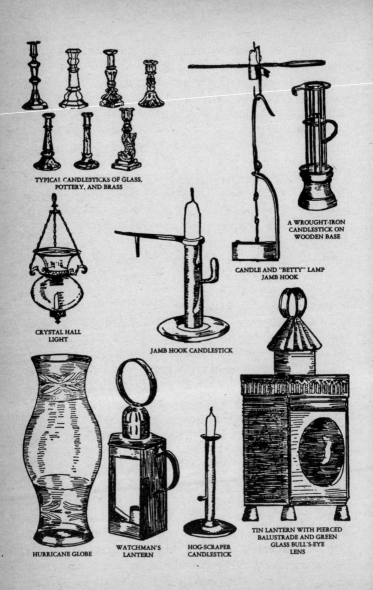

TYPICAL CANDLESTICKS OF GLASS,
POTTERY, AND BRASS

A WROUGHT-IRON
CANDLESTICK ON
WOODEN BASE

CRYSTAL HALL
LIGHT

JAMB HOOK CANDLESTICK

CANDLE AND "BETTY" LAMP
JAMB HOOK

HURRICANE GLOBE

WATCHMAN'S
LANTERN

HOG-SCRAPER
CANDLESTICK

TIN LANTERN WITH PIERCED
BALUSTRADE AND GREEN
GLASS BULL'S-EYE
LENS

sheet iron, pewter, brass, pottery, or even of glass. These molds were arranged in frames holding anywhere from a pair to three dozen. The molds were threaded with candlewicking and then poured full of hot wax from a spouted kettle. When cold and hard, the molds were plunged into hot water which loosened the molded candle and made removal from the mold quite easy.

Of course after 1680 there were professional chandlers, or candlemakers, at work and keeping shop in large towns. There was a candlemaker in Boston as early as 1634. He charged fourpence for a single candle which weighed, probably, four ounces. Today, when we say candles cost so much a pound, the price sounds cheap. But there was not much to a pound of candles; in some cases it was just one candle. If we compare the price paid for a pound of these lights with the wage paid to a workman of the same period we begin to understand why people got up with the sun and went to bed when it set. Of course we should keep in mind that most of the "living" in early American homes was done in the keeping room. Here the food was prepared, bread baked, sewing and reading done, and spinning, weaving, and other tasks carried out. There was always a fire going in the huge fireplace. When the fire was brisk, there was a great deal of light coming from the fireplace. This may well explain why, in most colonial lighting fixtures, there is evidence of effort to bring the light to a certain desired level or place—to focus it, as it were.

As time went on itinerant candlemakers toured the countryside, making candles for any who desired them made from home-saved fats. At times such itinerants would make enough candles to last a whole year—one to two thousand of them. Does the thought of two thousand candles startle you? Try illuminating your own home with five and a half candles a day. If we tried it

WHALE-OIL LAMP WITH
METAL SHADE

ASTRAL LAMP

BRASS CANDLESTICK WITH
METAL SHADE

DOUBLE CANDLESTICK WITH
METAL SHADE AND
WEIGHTED BASE

we'd be in the dark most of the time. Yet much fat had to be saved in order to provide enough to make two thousand candles. Used-fat conservation is no new thing in the American scene.

Candleholders while not absolutely necessary for burning a candle, are almost mandatory. Evidently our colonists thought so for they made, and had made for them, so many types, kinds, and varieties of candlesticks that tabulation is out of the question. The most primitive candlestick was an upright spike on a broad base, or on a flat disk which, in turn, was set at the top of an upright column. Needless to say, most household-size candles split when pushed down on the spike. The pricket-type candlestick demanded "fat" candles—the kind of candles that only rich people or churches could afford. Hence the pricket stick was not popular for home use. The socketed candlestick was the type almost universally used in the domestic scene. The common metal candlestick was usually made of thin sheet iron. A tube, approximately of candle size, fixed upright on a convex or concave iron base, sometimes with a ring handle, constituted the entire assembly. Later the tube was slotted, and a pusher with key raised or lowered the candle in the socket. These candleholders served the common man. If he could not afford a sheet-iron holder, he could make or buy a wooden holder from a wood turner for a few pennies. After common redware potteries were at work he could buy a pottery candlestick.

Fine artisans, merchants, and perhaps some well-to-do gentlemen had iron candlesticks of quite a different sort. These were of wrought iron—graceful, tall, and fitted with an adjustable crossarm. Shafts of these wrought-iron stands ended in a three-legged pedestal, often charmingly wrought. The crossarm, holding candle sockets, was also often decoratively wrought. Some of these candlestands are quite tall and are comparable to the modern bridge lamp. At times they were used for precisely the same purposes: to light up a card table or to provide a well-adjusted light for reading. The counterpart of these fine wrought-iron stands was also made of wood. These have turned shafts, heavy bases, and often the shaft is cut in the form of a wood screw on which the cross shaft turns and is adjusted to the height desired. Some of the crossarms on primitive wood stands of this type look like slimmed dumbbells in pairs. The heavy ends were bored to hold the candles.

The finest wood candlestands, fashioned of walnut, cherry, maple and, after 1750, of mahogany, have a circular shelf around the shaft about thirty inches above the base. This served as a table with light above it. Tradition has it that supper, in solo, was sometimes served on such candlestand tables. We do not doubt it. Neither can we doubt that such table stands served as worktables and as reading tables. They are quite fine and far from common as antiques today.

Worthy of mention here is the common iron type of candlestick known as the hog scraper. This unlovely term is honestly applied. The base, circular and convex, had quite a sharp edge. The lip of these sticks, where the candle is inserted, has a projection, bent to form a hook by which the stick could be hung on a chair rail or slat. The hog-scraping part was the base. Slaughtered hogs were scraped bare of bristles with the bases of these sticks, the cylinder of the stick serving as a handle for the scraper. Needless to say these sticks are quite sturdily made.

Metal shades for candlesticks, in the form of shields, reflectors, and cylinders, seem to have been in use from

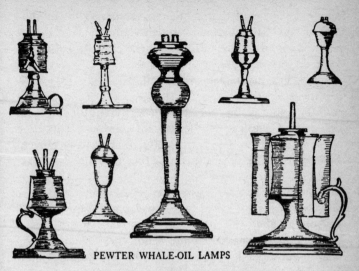

PEWTER WHALE-OIL LAMPS

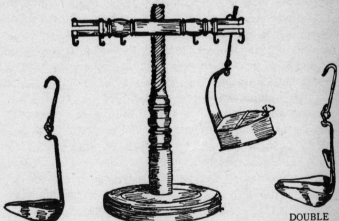

"BETTY"
LAMP

"BETTY" LAMP STAND WITH TIN
"BETTY" LAMP

DOUBLE
"BETTY"
LAMP

the first quarter of the eighteenth century. The counterpart of the Saint-Germain student lamp of the 1830s–1880s is found in shaded candlesticks of 1750–1800. The upright of the student-lamp candlestick is fixed to a large hollow base filled with sand. With this firm footing the single arm with its shade could be suspended from one side of the upright and at some distance from the shaft. Complete candlesticks of this particular type are now quite scarce; it is doubtful if they were ever in general use. They were in the nature of a specialty and a luxury.

Beyond the iron candlestick, in price, came the pewter candlestick. Pewter, originally developed by the Chinese and often called "tutenag" and sometimes "white brass," was in much favor for church candlesticks from the sixteenth century. Examples from the Netherlands and Flanders, shaped like slender Chinese vases, round or hexagonal in cross section, have been popular for some years as lamp bases. Electrified, they now serve as lamps in many homes. Most pewter candlesticks were formed by casting in metal molds. Brass candlesticks were both spun and cast. Brass was exceedingly scarce in the colonies. Even the clockmakers and the buttonmakers are known to have turned to brass kettles as their source of the metal. Hence we did not cast brass candlesticks in the round, or solid. We cast them hollow, in halves, and brazed them together. The brazing line on any brass item, whether candlestick, fire iron, or fire shovel handle, is an almost sure sign of colonial workmanship. However, the colonial artisans made but a small portion of the brass candlesticks sold and used in the colonies. Trade with English manufacturers was quite brisk. Lighting fixtures of quality were imported in great quantities, not only from England direct, but from Venice, France, and the Netherlands. Among our

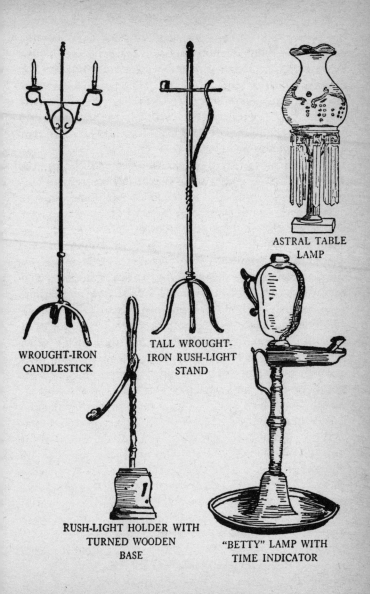

ASTRAL TABLE
LAMP

WROUGHT-IRON
CANDLESTICK

TALL WROUGHT-
IRON RUSH-LIGHT
STAND

RUSH-LIGHT HOLDER WITH
TURNED WOODEN
BASE

"BETTY" LAMP WITH
TIME INDICATOR

pictures are several taken directly from the illustrated catalogue of the Shelton Lamp Works of London and Liverpool. The items pictured were made between the years 1770 and 1830. Since the catalogue from which these pictures come was once used by a New York importing house, we may be sure this house imported and sold such lights. The catalogue has fifty-six engraved pages of pictures.

The ultimate in candlesticks is, of course, the candlestick of silver. It might seem reasonable to suppose that all our early American silversmiths, at some time or other, made candlesticks. But they didn't. Spoons, creamers, sugar basins, tankards, teapots, and such, yes, but very few candlesticks. Only the finest homes enjoyed them. When, however, the imitation silver known as Sheffield plate was invented by Bulsover in the eighteenth century, the equivalent of silver candlesticks could be had at half the price of pure silver. We made no Sheffield plate in this country although, it is said, several attempts to make it ended in failure, not because we didn't know how but because it was made more economically and to better advantage in Sheffield. In short, England mass-produced this ware. In stepping up production they could lower the price. Sheffield is basically a sandwich of two thin sheets of silver over a thick slab of copper or, rarely, a slab of tin. So faithful an imitation of solid silver could be made of this built-up metal that the English law required marking it as "Sheffield." Plate, of course, was the generic term for any ware made . of metal. Silver plate meant solid silver; tin plate meant solid tin; and so on. Sheffield plate, as a term, was not used to describe the process of making; it was used to designate the quality of the plate. It was Sheffield, hence not solid silver.

Luckily, we can also turn to the original catalogues of

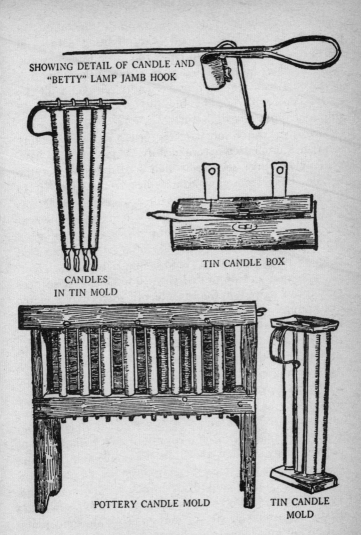

SHOWING DETAIL OF CANDLE AND
"BETTY" LAMP JAMB HOOK

CANDLES
IN TIN MOLD

TIN CANDLE BOX

POTTERY CANDLE MOLD

TIN CANDLE
MOLD

makers of Sheffield plate for exemplary illustrations of candlesticks, candelabra, and other lighting fixtures of top quality. To attempt to chart the various shapes and types of silver and Sheffield-plate candlesticks is another impossible task for the present work. We could fill the entire book with nothing but pictures and captions of different types of candlesticks.

Wall sconces for room lighting are quite a fascinating item in illuminating-fixture history. Many sconces have shallow hoodlike sections which served to protect the candle flame from downdrafts that would cause it to flicker. Some sconces were made to serve as reflectors and others to serve as "pictures" when the candle was lighted. The first type had many pieces of mirror glass set in a tile pattern, while the latter were of painted tole, or Pontypool ware, both being aristocratic terms for japanned and decorated sheet iron. The first sconces perhaps were used in the seventeenth century. Not many, but enough sheet-iron ones survive from this period to warrant the assumption that they were in fairly general use. The early sconces were all tall and narrow affairs, partaking of the quality of a niche for a single candle. As we progressed through the eighteenth century the wall sconce was made to accommodate two, three, and even four candles. The back piece was extended in size and varied in shape. Some black-tin and even sheet-iron sconces of this period are known, with small pieces of polished pewter laid on to act as reflectors. In one example there is a sheet of glass over the pewter inlays to prevent soiling and discoloration. Sconces of brass were made in limited numbers. Some sconces were made in pewter, some of silver, and some of Sheffield plate.

Candle- and lamp-trimming tools were quite common throughout our entire colonial and early federal period. Those most generally used were the Betty lamp pick,

LARD LAMP WITH
REFLECTOR

DOUBLE BULL'S-EYE
LIGHT

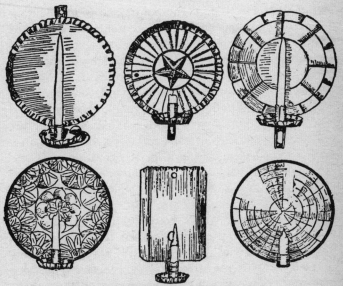

EARLY TIN, PEWTER, AND MIRROR SCONCES

the snuffer, and the cone extinguisher. The two last named were used with candles: the snuffer to trim the wick of the candle while burning, the cone to extinguish the flame without danger of scattering hot wax. Sometimes the snuffers, of brass, steel, pewter, silver, or Sheffield plate, were fitted with a special holder, looking like a candlestick base but with a box to hold the snuffer, point down. Conical extinguishers were often made a part of a candlestick ensemble whether of brass, pewter, silver, or Sheffield plate. Extension snuffers for use with candles in hurricane shades or candles burning in chandeliers were made to extend two feet or more. These are excessively rare and were probably a unique luxury.

If the use of candles, rushlights, and allied lighting devices was responsible for the accumulation of tons of fixtures in our American scene, the accumulation was as nothing compared to the mass of lamps that were purchased and used from the middle of the eighteenth century. It may well be that Benjamin Franklin, pondering over candles in his father's candle shop in Boston, invented the double-wick candle. Whether it was his idea, or whether it was someone else's, doesn't matter. It was a good idea. Within it lay the germ of the greatest single lamp and lighting invention in several thousand years. Let us first consider the basics involved. Two flames, burning side by side, permit a draft of air between them. Air is necessary to complete combustion. The two-wick candle, never successful, suggested the two-wick lamp. That was successful. Then, in 1783, a Swiss scientist, Argand, conceived the idea of a round wick with a draft of air around the outside and through the center. This invention, in one swoop, pushed better lighting into prominence. All that was required was that a prospective customer see an Argand lamp burning and note what he could see with its light.

He was ready to sell his candlesticks, sconces, and all
else, if he had to, in order to have an Argand light. The
Argand light literally prodded hundreds and even thousands of lampmakers, metalsmiths, and others into
thinking about lamps and lighting from the standpoint
of better, cheaper light. Soon there were Argand sconces,
Argand chandeliers, Argand burners for every place and
every type of lamp. Some of the wicks were no bigger
around than a thimble end. Some were as large as a
dollar. By 1790 America had scores of lampmaking
shops. Within two decades we had mass-production
factories.

Rainy-day amusements of the sort suggested to children can be indulged in by antiquarians to answer many
questions we have in our mind on certain subjects. Once
we put down the population of our nation at the end
of the Revolution. Three million was the figure. Families,
of course, were then bigger on the average, so we divided the population by five to estimate the number of
houses that must have been standing. Then we multiply
that by four to estimate the number of principal rooms.
The figure is 2,400,000. Suppose the average was four
candlesticks to a room, six chairs, one table, one mirror,
one set of fire tools and andirons, one chest, one bed.
That predicated almost ten million candlesticks, close to
15,000,000 chairs, and so on. This isn't so silly as it
sounds. In our files we have several hundred original
bills for furniture, lamps, mirrors, and other items dated
between 1755 and 1775. These bills were made out to
Edward Shippen of Philadelphia and Lancaster. To look
at them in light of today's buying of the average well-to-
do gentleman, one would think Mr. Shippen was buying
like a drunken sailor. He bought chairs by the half
dozen and dozen. He had chairs repaired by the dozen.
He purchased lamps in pairs and fours.

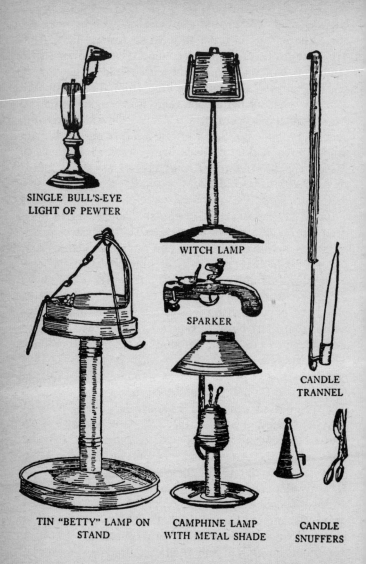

SINGLE BULL'S-EYE
LIGHT OF PEWTER

WITCH LAMP

SPARKER

CANDLE
TRANNEL

TIN "BETTY" LAMP ON
STAND

CAMPHINE LAMP
WITH METAL SHADE

CANDLE
SNUFFERS

There was one factory in Philadelphia credited with making ten thousand lamps a day in 1840. Another in New York was making five thousand a day. As our new nation grew (and how it grew!) decade after decade, the figures for lamp ownership doubled and tripled. Camphene, a most explosive burning fluid made of alcohol and turpentine that made a brilliant light, put better light, and a terrific fire hazard, into several million American homes and cottages. Lard-oil and whale-oil lamps, some with large magnifying lenses on either side of the flame, and a host of other patented open-flame lamps, were quite common during the first thirty or more years of our federal period. This great use of open-flame lamps only pointed to the need for better lamps equipped with shades, chimneys, moons, or globes. Among the open-flame lamps is that engaging variant called the petticoat, or sparking, lamp. The lamp didn't spark, and didn't give much more than a spark of light, but it is called a sparking lamp because it was the ideal lamp for sparking—the sweet term our grandsires and grandmothers used to designate what we call petting, wrestling, and necking. Another cute, quaint, and quite inadequate lamp was the sheet-iron shaded device with a mica window.

It may sound a bit curious, unless one is familiar with the weird ways of evolution in common things, but the endeavor to make lamps out of candlesticks which started about 1790 established a technique of lamp-reservoir making that is used to this day. It happened in this way: some genius noted the number of candlesticks then in use and figured that if he could make a lamp, complete with reservoir and burner, that could be put in a candlestick, he would make a fortune. He made his lamp reservoir with a stump or peg, in the bottom. It fitted into the candle socket of a candlestick. Thou-

Engravings of lamps sold by American importers, taken directly from the catalog of the Shelton Lamp Works, London and Birmingham, 1770–1830.

sands of fluid-burning lamp reservoirs are made that way today and fitted into socketed bases. The first peg lamps were made of metal. Then they were made of glass. What is not said here, in words, in respect of other and later lamps of the kerosene period, is omitted only because to attempt to say it would extend this chapter to unreasonable limits.

At one time in American history a round lantern with a conical top, with small holes punched in a decorative design all over the body and sometimes in the top, hung in almost every barn and shed. These lanterns were popular and in most general use about 1836. Somewhere, somebody gave this lantern the magic name of "Paul Revere." We may be quite sure that this lantern is not the type hung in the tower of the Old North Church to indicate to Revere whether the British were going by land or by sea. It is, rather, the type of lantern most useful as a fire carrier. These perforated lanterns were made as late as 1910. They are one of the major items listed in the Philadelphia *Tinsmiths' Book of Prices,* issued in 1838. As a quaint relic they are quite engaging; as lanterns, they aren't worth the match it takes to light one. They are, actually, only a poor relation of the first lanthorn, or light-in-horn case.

Peeled ox horn of the sort once used for watch crystals, window lights, and other transparency purposes, was the window material used around a lamp or candle. The framing was of metal. These early lanthorns were round, with three "windows" and a door all fitted with horn. The roof of the lanthorn was conical and often had air holes in the form of dormer windows. "A little transparent house for a light" is an accurate description of these first portable lamps. "Moons" were drum-shaped lanthorns with large faces looking, of course, like moons. The same term was applied to glass globes in which a

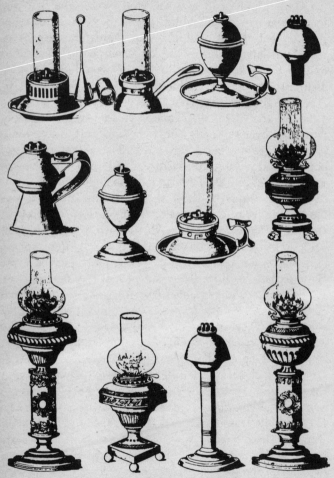

More lamps from the catalog of the Shelton Lamp Works. The original catalog contains over 50 pages of illustrations such as these. All are lamps sold in the colonies in the Federal era, and used by the hundreds of thousands in American homes.

lamp or candle was placed. Both kinds of moons were for outdoor use. Moon was the first name given to sedan chair and carriage lamps. Cressets were baskets of strap-iron work in which combustibles were fired to provide light. Street cressets were the first street lights. Boston had cressets burning at its principal street corners in 1690. It was the task of the watchman to keep the cressets supplied with fuel during the night hours. In 1772 Boston purchased several hundred street-lighting fixtures from a British firm. These were oil-burning lamps in large glassed boxes set on posts. By the year 1792 the United States was producing its own street lamps and lamps of many other sorts and kinds.

The use of glass in lampmaking was tried as early as 1750, at Quincy, Massachusetts. Glass lamps and candle-sticks were made. In the year 1780 lamps were made of glass at Temple, New Hampshire. At Sandwich, Massa-chusetts, innumerable lamps and candlesticks, notably the dolphin, were made by Deeming Jarves's factory. Lamps, when made for either sperm oil or patented fluid, differed not at all in the reservoir and support con-struction but only in burner details. Beautiful lamps in overlay glass were made at Sandwich.

It is perhaps unfortunate in one sense and in another sense quite fortunate for discriminating collectors that far too much interest has been displayed in part years to kerosene-burning lamps of the Victorian era. This focus-ing of attention on quite latecomers in the parade of early lighting has blacked out, so to speak, the early lamps of our federal era. Far finer lamps were made in this earlier period—lamps more at home with any interior furnished in the true antique, with objects made before 1830. Hanging lanterns for halls and hanging lamps for any rooms in the house were produced by a score or more of reputable makers, all of whom advertised their wares before 1830. Certain of the lamps pictured with this chapter are captioned to explain, as briefly as possible, their construction and method of combustion. Among these will be found types of almost every lamp generally available now in antiques shops. We have not given attention to any types of lamp now so excessively rare that examples can be found only in museums or in noted private collections.

Chapter XVI

MIRRORS

SEVENTEENTH-CENTURY mirrors fall into two broad categories—fine and poor—based upon the quality of the glass used and having nothing to do with the framing. Depending upon circumstances and conditions prevailing in the colonies, we may find a fine mirror surviving in a poor frame and a poor mirror surviving in a fine frame. Fine mirrors were made of plate glass, relatively free from surface flaws which, when the glass was silvered, would distort the reflection. Poor mirrors were made from crown glass, the thin and sometimes visibly corrugated panes cut from a circular crown of blown glass. Plate glass in the seventeenth century was cast upon beds of polished marble or metal. Each piece was beveled by hand, perhaps with a tool somewhat like a marver, while the sheet of glass was still plastic. The method of making plate glass seems to have been the exclusive secret of Italian glassmakers of Venice and Murano until about the middle of the seventeenth century. Then in France and in England factories, or studios, for making it were established. In England the Duke of Buckingham set up a plate-glass works at Vauxhall, in 1662. Prior to that time all of England's fine mirror glass was imported. The silvering of fine mirrors was accomplished by coating the glass with sheets of tin foil made to adhere to the glass with a film of mercury. Crown glass mirrors were seldom silvered with tin foil and mercury; some sort of amalgam or paint was used. Various recipes were in favor, invloving lead, tin, mercury, pitch, varnish, and some secret ingredients. Any pane of crown glass is apt to show sections of wavy, circular lines, originally a part of the great circular crown in which the glass was blown. A large bubble of glass was blown and cut from the pipe when the pontil rod was affixed opposite the blowpipe. This left on the pontil a bubble of hot, soft glass looking like a huge fish bowl. Spinning the pontil caused the bowl to expand and finally spread into a large circular sheet. This was a "crown" of glass. When annealed in a special gloryhole in the glass furnace, it was cooled and cut into panes. The least useful pane was the center one on which a thick gob of glass remained, together with the scar of the pontil rod. This was known as the bull's eye. It was used mainly in overdoor lights, in lanterns, and where light but not vision was needed in window or door. Even crown glass was far from cheap. It is said that print and picture framers, a craft closely allied to mirror making, developed the habit of cropping print margins and close framing in order to conserve glass. Crown glass made poor mirrors. Beveled plate glass, backed with tin foil, made fine mirrors. The bevel is so flat as to defy detection by the eye. One must feel it to be aware there is a bevel on it.

Because of high price, neither fine mirrors nor poor mirrors were common in colonial days prior to 1700. There are some records of American glass factories in Virginia, New Jersey, and Massachusetts attempting to make mirror glass, and records of some attempts to start mirror-glass factories. In the late 1730s artisans who could silver mirrors advertised their services in several cities and towns. These men may have silvered flat glass of colonial production but chances are their activity was confined largely to restoring and resilvering existing pieces of plate glass and of silvering sheets of glass imported plain. One thing is quite sure, the name "mirror maker" in the seventeenth century could be applied to the maker of the glass plate, the man who silvered it, and to the man who framed it. Rarely, indeed, were any two of these functions performed by one man or group of men.

In the earlier days, when mirrors were made mostly of polished metal, it is conceivable that the artisan made the mirror from first to last—casting the plate, polishing it, and framing it. Early English manuscripts picture the shops of such mirror makers. The products offered for sale are small hand mirrors, not "looking glasses." After the general use of glass in making mirrors the quite logical popular term for these mirrors was "looking glass."

So much for the material, silvered glass, that makes the mirror. To most of us it is the complete, framed item of furniture or home furnishing only that deserved the name of mirror or looking glass. The earliest complete mirrors used in the colonies seem to have been framed in a combination of Italian and Flemish styles. "Olive wood molding, inlaid and otherwise embellished, made into almost square frames, surmounted by a cresting," would be a fair description of the basic type. But the variations of that type almost beggar description. The cresting was sometimes pierced and sometimes painted, inlaid, or carved. The molding narrowed, the cresting festooned downward over the sides of the mirror, and additional reverse cresting was added to the bottom molding. In short, the seventeenth-century mirror, by a simple evolutionary process of beautification, developed into the William and Mary and Queen Anne styles and, finally, into the Georgian style often wrongly called Chippendale.

Many New England mirrors bespeak home workmanship. Reduced to the most simple form, it consisted of a small flat piece of wood, usually pine, upon which the mirror was mounted and held in place by small strips of wood molding overlapping the glass and pegged to the back board. At top, bottom, and sides the back board protruded beyond the molding and was sometimes roughly shaped to look like crestings. This crude mirror filled the need for the New Englander at the time when the wealthier settlers of Virginia were importing the glasses of Vauxhall.

It is interesting to note that by 1650, in spite of the luxury status of mirrors, our colonial records indicate that we used more mirrors per capita than did England. Inventories mention "walnut-tree glasses," "looking glasses," "mirrors," "olive wood glasses," and so on.

By 1710 mirror styles reveal a glass taller and less wide than formerly, in slightly molded cross-banded frames. The tops are shaped with cyma and ogee curves, mitered at the joinings, as were the frames proper. In some examples of this type a cresting is carried beyond the upper edge of the frame and is jig-sawed or carved. Metal brackets for candles were sometimes affixed to the frame. Occasionally we find the entire frame gilded.

The mirror with pierced, crested top, commonly called "jig saw," in various forms and sizes persisted in America for more than a century. The cruder farmhouse or pioneer mirrors were simply constructed, the frame being one piece of wood, jigsawed at the top and bottom or only at the top. When the maker did not have a jig saw he carved or cut the openwork with chisels and knives. The opening was grooved at the back to permit the glass to sink partially into the frame while the molding about the front of the opening prevented it from falling

COURTING MIRROR

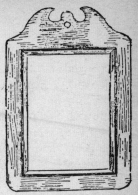

EARLY PINE MIRROR

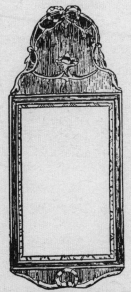

MIRROR OF THE LATTER
HALF OF THE SEVEN-
TEENTH CENTURY

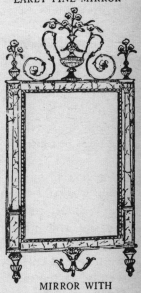

MIRROR WITH
MARBLE FRAME

out. The back was then sealed with a single sheet of board extending over the opening.

The more pretentious mirrors of this same type were constructed in a somewhat similar fashion but more meticulously. Expert cabinetmakers rounded the corners of the molding and embellished the inner line of the frame with gilding. The center of the cresting was often broken with a cutout circle into which was set a gilded gesso eagle or three-plume motif.

Between 1725 and 1745 a wide tripartite or three-pane mirror to hang over, or rest on, mantels was introduced. The frame was wood, gilded, ornamented with architectural details, scrolled, or plain. The joinings of the three pieces of glass were covered with a molding. These over-mantel mirrors seem to have been more common in the great manor houses of Maryland and Virginia than in New England.

During this same period the first dressing glasses appeared on the scene. Such glasses were attached horizontally by screws to turned or squared uprights standing on a box fitted with several small drawers. Many of these mirror frames were veneered, others inlaid, and some had jig-sawed or shaped cresting. The dressing glass, we gather from letters and wills, was a popular and well-received gift.

About 1745 American craftsmen made a rococo gilt mirror that so closely simulated the Italian mirrors of the time that only by minutely detailed examination can we discern the differences. In outline they were irregular though still retaining rectangular shapes. A wooden frame made the foundation upon which a restless arrangement of scrolls and foliage was built up in gesso— a composition plaster worked on a foundation of wood and bent wire. The irregular shape of these mirrors

TYPICAL
JIGSAW MIRRORS

on the inner as well as the outer side generally prevented use of beveled glass. In some, however, the glass is beveled to shape. In these examples we may be quite sure that the frame was made to fit the mirror and not the mirror made to fit the frame.

The next stage of mirror style development gave us probably as fine a mirror as any our colonial craftsmen produced. It has a broken pediment upon an architecturally detailed architrave. Below the top is a molding with projected square corners that carry down the sides and into a scrolled bottom apron. The inner edges of the molding are delicately carved and gilded, as is also the narrow molding directly adjacent to the glass. The architrave is carved with the egg-and-dart or other motifs, and gilded. The scroll of the broken arch is gilded and ends in a small rosette with pendent leaves, at times also gilded. A molded plasterwork fillet is suspended from the corner of the square molding at either side. Below the pediment some of these mirrors display carved and gilded ornaments. In the center of the broken arch we find gilded urns, shell, eagles, and Prince of Wales' plumes. The wealth of delicate carving and the cautious use of gilt against a beautiful piece of cherry, walnut, or mahogany veneer give a beauty to these mirrors that is unrivaled by any others.

During the middle years of the eighteenth century, when Wren's architecture was introducing a new spirit into the interiors of America, we find mirrors becoming an integral part of wall paneling, with refined architectural detail and carving. These are known as pier glasses. Pier mirror designs from the work of Sir Christopher Wren and Robert Adam were widely copied in the colonies.

An interesting and lovely mirror that seems to have

CHIPPENDALE GILT MIRROR

ORNATE CHIPPENDALE MIRROR

A GILT MIRROR

been comparatively common during the latter years of the eighteenth century is known as the filigree looking glass. The ornamentation was made of gesso upon a wire foundation. Rectangular in shape, the molding of the frame, often carved, ran clear around the glass. At the crest stood an urn from which extended scrolls of leafy branches and flowers. The urn was often fluted and there were medallions and rosettes in the floral scrolls.

In the American mirrors of the middle Georgian period, often called Chippendale, we find a lack of restraint that often gives a quality of ostentation. Usually of gilt and rococo in their treatment, they stand in sharp contrast to the more severe architectural styles which preceded them. "C" curves are prominent; vases, medallions, scrolls, ribbons, shells, pheasants, temples, and fretwork are used with a wide variety of woods and finishes. Between the frame proper and the mirror glass smaller pieces of mirror, sometimes in color, were often inserted.

One jig-saw mirror style developed in this country differs from all others of the same class in that the scrolls employed curve toward the outside of the frame and the "C" formed thereby always faces the glass.

Other mirrors found in many New England seaport towns are commonly called "courting mirrors." These are of Chinese origin and were brought here by seamen as gifts. At best they are relics of the introduction of an interesting, exotic note in early furnishings. Owing to the abundant use of small segments of painted glass making up the frames, courting mirrors were packed in small, flat boxes for safety. In these boxes they usually remained when hung on the wall. At the top of most courting mirrors is a geometric shape of three or five

CONVEX GIRANDOLE MIRROR

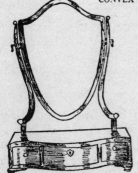

SERPENTINE-FRONT DRESS-
ING GLASS

SWELL-FRONT DRESSING GLASS

sides forming a cresting. The containing box does not follow this shape at the top, but remains rectangular. Floral or geometric designs of varying degrees of crudeness and perfection were painted upon the back of the border glasses. These mirrors may well be a cheap form of the Persian "wedding mirror" which is, of course, of oriental design with a glass-inlaid border.

Another form of mirror sometimes found in seaport towns is the Bilbao. In this mirror the frame is made entirely of sheets of colored marble. On the sides are marble columns with gilded finials and feet, and at the top is a large medallion or urn supported by gilded scrolls of leaves and flowers. These mirrors, supposedly, came from Portugal.

The reversion to certain classical forms because of French influence following the American Revolution caused a great change in the mirror styles. All the flowing line of the jig-saw and Chippendale glasses was consigned to oblivion and replaced with severe, formal neoclassicism. Black and gold predominate over wood finishes and add to the formal atmosphere. Two mirror types of this period, the girandole and the tabernacle, became quite popular. The tabernacle mirror, often called Sheraton—which it isn't—literally flooded the country.

The girandole was a circular mirror framed in a deep molding of gilt and black. The fillet of black ran next to the glass and in the hollow deep gilt molding the supposedly symbolic thirteen balls were placed at regular intervals. The top was surmounted by an eagle, flame, or dolphin. In some cases, where the eagle was used, strings of prisms were suspended from his beak and carried to candle sconces that were inserted in the side of the frame.

The tabernacle mirror frame is rectangular with beveled cornice and pilasters superimposed upon the sides. A third or less of the mirror space, at the top, is partitioned off and filled with a painting on glass or a solid piece of gilded wood displaying carved fruit, foliage, or other motifs. This mirror developed from the French *trumeau* mirror—a form of pier mirror imitating a doorframe with decorative overdoor panel. On a few rare examples the eagle and thirteen stars are symbolically painted or carved. On the natural wood, painted and stained tabernacle mirrors, and sometimes on gilded examples, small acorns are set into and below the cornice. Later, perhaps within a few years, gilded balls replaced the acorn and side pilasters became mere strips of molding. The better made frames displayed classical columns in the half-round, or fluted, rope-turned or plain strips applied to the basic frame.

By 1815 the tabernacle mirror went into mass production in almost every village and town. Nearly every newspaper of the day carried advertisements of mirror makers, looking-glass makers, and molding factories that made mirrors. In Cincinnati one mirror factory is said to have turned out a thousand a day. In this period there were tabernacle-type mirrors made in sizes ranging from sixteen to thirty-six inches high. The very cheap ones had grooved molding all around with blocks at the corners, trimmed with applied rosettes. Most of these were of cherry wood, or soft woods, stained. The better quality factory product displayed some gilding or bronzing. Production of tabernacle mirrors by the hundreds of thousands, and perhaps by the millions, continued to about 1835 when a new type of mirror entered the scene—a mirror belonging with, and as unlovely as most of the furniture now designated as "Empire." Yet, somehow, most of the Empire mirrors missed being altogether bad and some of them are quite lovely. They

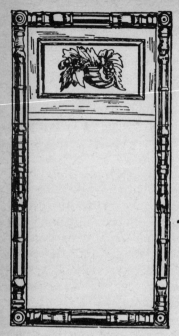

MIRROR WITH PAINTED
DECORATION

TABERNACLE MIRROR

are, generally, to be described as four pieces of heavy, split bulbous turning, meeting at large corner blocks and decorated with gesso applications on the turning and on the corner blocks. These mirrors were gilded and bronzed. Where there is a combination of bright burnished yellow gilding and darker gilt bronzing, the effect is quite charming. They were also made in a variety of sizes, some of the smaller ones have turning as delicate as the front arm supports of Windsor chairs, while the larger ones boast turnings as heavy as those on the bedposts of this period.

Cheval glasses, or "horse mirrors," of the late eighteenth and early nineteenth centuries seem to have lacked popularity in the United States. These glasses are large and hang between a pair of upright supports between which the mirror can be tilted. Because no one state produced an unusual mirror style we can make no material geographic differentiations. The styles of any period were made and used in any colony existing at that period. But most certainly we have records of unusual mirror production in certain colonies and states. When outstanding, mention of such production is made in the chapters devoted to the various colonies and states.

Chapter XVII

GLASS

IF YOU ever visit Jamestown, Virginia, you can see some examples of glass beads dug up from the site of the first glass house ever built on these shores. The date of the glass house is problematic; the furnace may have been a part of the famed first brickyard. But most certainly this effort at glassmaking was started within a few years of the settling of Jamestown, and for a very specific commercial reason—to make glass beads—money with which to buy lands and goods from the native American Indians. That is why coin collectors can call this venture, not a glass house, but the first colonial mint. It may be that bottles were made at Jamestown. Perhaps other utilitarian wares were also fashioned, but no matter what was made, there is no remaining Jamestown glass to collect.

Caspar Wistar, a native of the Netherlands, started the first really important glassmaking venture in the colonies in Salem County, New Jersey, about 1739. Some authorities have tried to classify Wistar as a German glassmaker named Wüstar, and his wares as German glass. A great German glass authority burst this canard very prettily when he disclosed that no family named Wistar or Wüstar had ever lived at or near the birthplace attributed to him by our experts, and that the glass made by Wistar was in no sense German. The German expert classed Wistar wares as exemplary of Netherlands glass.

Caspar Wistar selected Salem County as the site of his glass house because of the readily available abundance of fuel and sand. In addition he had the benefit of a waterway to ship his glass to ports of the Delaware and to Philadelphia, his major retail market. Wistar employed four glassblowers named Haltar, Halton, Crijsmijer, and Wentzell. The first glass made by Wistar is utterly Dutch in character, style, and shape. It was crude but it bore also the surface application of wavy lines of glass, typical of Dutch forms of decoration. If Wistar glass is crude, it is also distinctive. In the paler shades of green and blue it offers unbelievably delicate, clear colors.

Wistar was the first American glassmaker to make bicolored glass by fusing two colors in the blowing and developing waved and whorled designs. This, too, is in the tradition of the contemporaneous glasswares of the Netherlands. The colored combinations used are emerald green and opaque white, clear glass with a tawny tinted blue, green glass with bluish-white glass, and amber with clear white. It is doubtful whether any dark blue glass was made at the Wistar factory. One characteristic of Wistar glass is the thin thread of glass wound spirally around the necks of pitchers and around the tops of bowls. Another specialty was the waved design achieved by coating a finished piece with a thin film, which was drawn over the surface of the original blowing to form the design.

Certain of the Wistar pieces have a crimped footing. This crimping, while characteristic of Wistar glass, was used by other glassmakers in south Jersey, including the famous factory at Millville. Wistar also made large and small glass balls and produced the first flint glass made in America. His factory made crown window glass, lamp glasses (lampshades and globes), bottles of all sizes from carafe to snuff, condiment pots, bowls, pitchers, and drinking glasses.

Much glassware now attributed to Wistar may have been made in other Jersey glasshouses. The Sanger brothers who had worked for Wistar opened a glass factory at Glassboro, New Jersey, in 1775. This venture remained in operation until 1837. It was then purchased by Thomas H. Whitney and became the Whitney Glass Works. It may come as something of a surprise even to collectors of Jersey glass to know that the factory founded by the Sangers in 1775 eventually became the Owens Bottle Company of Toledo, Ohio, where Michael J. Owens developed the Owens bottle blowing machine. At the Whitney Glass Works were made the famous "booze" bottles in the shape of a log cabin, the beehive and cider barrel inkwells of the Harrison campaign of 1840, and the equally important gourd-shaped Jenny Lind flasks.

Other New Jersey glassmakers included the Lee Glass Works of Port Elizabeth, established about 1800 and operated under various managements until 1885, when it was abandoned. Jonathan Haines had a glass factory at Clementon, established about 1800, which remained in operation intermittently until 1825.

James Lee, one of the partners of the Port Elizabeth Glass Works, established a factory at Millville, New Jersey, in 1806. This finally became the Whitall-Tatum Glass Works in 1857. This factory is today a large producer of glass containers. Antiquarian interest in the Millville glass factory is owing to the fact that here was first produced one of the most famous paperweights in the world—the Millville Rose. Tremendous quantities of paperweights were made in Millville from about 1860 to 1910. In 1863 Whitall-Tatum set up a wooden mold department and commercial production of paperweights

Wistarberg glass of early type, pure Dutch in style, quality, and workmanship. Wistar, for many years, was promoted as a German glassmaker and his glassware as German-type glass. This was a pure fabrication. Wistar was Dutch, his workmen were Dutch, and his glassware is recognized as of Dutch type and style. Examples shown here are bicolored with opaque glass over the transparent.

began. According to one expert commentator and researcher on Millville paperweights, the early weights were quite crude, of the fountain and swirl designs. Then came the Millville Lily and others containing potted flowers, horses, dogs, and boats. About 1880 Ralph Barber, one of the Stagers, and Michael Kane were the master craftsmen at Millville. Ralph Barber was once credited with producing all the Millville Rose paperweights, but it is now believed other master craftsmen produced similar weights after Barber had perfected the technique of its making. Millville Rose paperweights are known in white, yellow, pink, and deep rose colors, some with stems and some without. At this plant were also made the Home Sweet Home, Friendship, and Masonic symbol paperweights. Millville also produced glass objects for home use and decoration.

New York, or rather New Amsterdam, had a glass furnace as early as 1645, when Everett Duykink is recorded as setting up a business. Johan Smedes had a glasshouse in operation in the 1660s. The Glass House Company, formed in the 1750s by Loderwyk Bamper, Matthew Earnest, Samuel Bayard, and Christian Hertel, was in operation until the mid-1760s. Bayard & Company were making glass at New Windsor, Ulster County, until 1785.

At Hamilton, New York, Leonard de Neufville and others had a glass factory in operation from the early 1780s to 1791. The Rensselaer Glass Works at Sand Lake operated from 1806 to 1853. The Utica works and others in northern New York State vied with New York City and Brooklyn houses in producing utilitarian wares. Hobbes of New York City was famed for cut glasswares from 1820 to 1840. Gilliland made fine flint glass at Brooklyn, in 1823–63.

The production of the early and late glasshouses of

Clear green Wistar glass, hand blown and beautifully formed. Such examples, while occasionally still found, are now in the category of rare American glass.

New York State ran to a very high total. Identification of the product of each house is largely a matter of high professional knowledge or expert opinion. It may well be that Bamper glass was made in the Dutch techniques that were used by Wistar in New Jersey. We may be misnaming Wistar as Bamper and vice versa.

We can leave identification and the squabbles over who is right and who is wrong to the professional experts in this field. The more expert the experts become the less squabbling is done and the more identification resolves itself into designation by "type" of glass rather than outright attribution to a specific factory.

It was in Lancaster County, Pennsylvania, that America's most famous antique glassware was produced by William Henry Stiegel who, arriving a penniless German immigrant, found America a magnificent land of opportunity. His glass factory, built in 1765 to boom a new town laid out as a speculative venture, produced glassware that is today worth at least its weight in silver and which, on more than one occasion, has sold for its weight in gold. It is, of course, only the fine colored blown glass made at the Stiegel works that bring excessively high prices. This glassware was but a small fraction of the total output of Stiegel's factory. He produced all kinds of blown glassware of white transparent variety—ordinary household glassware, bottles, flasks, and apothecaries' vials. Nearly all Stiegel glass, in type and form, is in imitation of English Bristol glass. Some attempts at imitating Venetian and Swedish glass were made. Some enameled glass similar to Swiss wares was also made.

Stiegel, however, was not the only fine glass made in Pennsylvania. In 1771 the Philadelphia Glass Works was established. In 1804 this factory was renamed the Kensington Glass Works. In 1833 it was under the control of Thomas W. Dyott and renamed the Dyottville

Once all of this glass would have been called Stiegel. Now the best we can do is to call it "Stiegel type." The enamel-decorated pieces are in imitation of Swiss glass of the same period. The tulip engraved flask and covered rummer are after Swedish types of glass, while the balance of the examples here pictured are in the Bristol English tradition.

Glass Works. Previous to 1825 the Kensington Glass Works made bottles and general utilitarian glasswares; after 1825 the now most important production was historic flasks of many kinds. The Schuylkill Glass Works was established at Philadelphia in 1780. This plant made flint glassware up to about 1820.

In 1797 Craig and O'Hara established a glassmaking enterprise at Pittsburgh which marked the beginning of the westward movement of our glass industry. Craig and O'Hara were making exceptionally fine glassware by 1800. The New Geneva Glass Works, established in 1797 by four Swiss glassblowers who had worked at Amelung's New Bremen Glass Works in Maryland, together with Messrs. Gallatin and Richardson, made tablewares, bottles, and window glass. In 1808 Bakewell & Company established a glassworks at Pittsburgh for the production of fine cut and engraved tablewares. The production rivaled the work of famed English and Irish glassmakers of the same period. In 1825 Bakewell began experiments in pressed-glass production. By 1860 Pittsburgh and other western Pennsylvania pressed-glass production had captured most of the American market. The glass factories at Sandwich and other eastern centers were hard pressed to hold their own against Pittsburgh competition. It was the production of fine glassware in and around Pittsburgh that caused glassmakers to enter the Ohio territory and set up new glass factories.

Maryland can boast of its New Bremen, or Amelung, glassware, made at the first foreign-owned factory in the United States of America. It was in 1784 that John Frederick Amelung of Bremen, Germany, established a glassworks at New Bremen, Frederick County. German capitalists financed the venture. Benjamin Crocker of Baltimore was in Bremen when the project was planned. He influenced the choice for his native state of Mary-

Stiegel-type covered bowls. The upper bowl of a gorgeous blue is perhaps accurately identified as Stiegel. It is doubtful whether the swan finial covered sugar bowl was ever made by Stiegel. It is most likely a piece of New England glass, perhaps from Sandwich.

land. A sum equal to ten thousand pounds was subscribed and the glass factory built. Workmen were brought over from Germany. Letters of endorsement were written by Franklin, Adams, William Paca, and Charles Carroll, all of whom were anxious to have this new glass factory become a success. The drawing of European capital to these shores was considered something of an achievement.

The manufactory at first was quite successful. It produced a tremendous amount of glass much of which, for many years, was mistakenly called Stiegel. This error of attribution stemmed from a belief current in antiques circles up to 1914 that any old glass with a rough mark on the bottom was Stiegel. Unfortunately, the New Bremen venture came to an end in 1795. It simply could not compete with Bristol glass, which could be laid down on the docks of Baltimore for less money than Amelung could be loaded on wagons at Fredericktown. However, during its short life the Amelung factory produced hundreds of thousands of examples of some of the finest glass ever made in America—Maryland glass—but made in the best glass traditions of Germany, Switzerland, the Netherlands, Sweden, Venice, and Bristol.

Ohio was hardly in process of general settlement before attempts were made to set up glasshouses within the borders of the new state. In fact, all kinds of manufacturing were fostered and encouraged because, while the rich farm lands inevitably would draw agricultural settlers, city and town dwellers had to have employment. Of course a farmer wanted pottery, glassware, furniture, textiles, and other necessities available at the nearest store, trading post, or town. Consequently Ohio was literally a beehive of budding industry during the first forty years of the nineteenth century. This history of Ohio glass production and the story of its glassware

Rare examples of Sandwich glass, including two candlesticks, one in dolphin shape, an apple paperweight, a pair of lamps, two vases, and two salt cellars. All of these examples, with the exception of the paperweight, fall in the category of pressed glass.

are just as fascinating as the unbelievable story of Cincinnati furniture production.

The researches of Mrs. Rhea Mansfield Knittle establish beyond shadow of doubt that glassmaking started at Zanesville, Ohio, in 1815. Under various managements the Zanesville factory produced blown glass and blown molded glassware as well as historic and decorative flasks in green, amber, olive, yellow, and transparent white. Patterned molded wares were made and a marked glass, identifying Zanesville as the point of production, is to be found in the category of bottles and flasks.

At Mantua in Portage County, originally a part of the Western Reserve, a Connecticut Yankee established a glassworks in 1821. Another glass factory was started in Steubenville about 1830. Glass production continued at Steubenville until one of the factories became a mass producer of goblets and tumblers—one of the largest in the nation.

Perhaps the most widely known Massachusetts antique is Sandwich glass. This ware, produced by Deming Jarves at the Boston and Sandwich Glass Company, falls into two broad categories—blown glass and pressed glass. The blown glass may be free blown or blown mold. The pressed glass, some of it the popular lacy Sandwich, has an antiques value now anywhere from ten to two hundred times its original price. Sandwich pressed glass was cheap glass when it was made. It came out of the pressing machine like so many pieces of plastic from a continuous molding machine.

Sandwich blown glass in its various forms was, before 1920, often wrongly attributed to Stiegel and was sold for the product of that earlier glassworks. Which, of course, indicates that Sandwich blown glass was made in various colors and in many shapes similar to the Stiegel product. Both plants, in fact, imitated English

Bristol glass. The New England Glass Company, incorporated in 1818, was in operation for some seventy years. In its early days the company made much glass. The plant finally became the Libby Glass Company. Those desirous of knowing the whole story of Massachusetts glass are referred to Laura Woodside Watkins's *Cambridge Glass*, Ruth Webb Lee's *Sandwich Glass*, and *American Glass* by George S. and Helen McKearin.

In the McKearin book (which should be broken up into three separate volumes because of its definity and wealth of information compressed into 622 large pages) there is ample evidence, geographically speaking, that every colony at one time or other had a glassmaking factory. In upper New York State, in Connecticut, New Hampshire, and other states, the ventures and the glasses made are fairly well known and tabulated. Lesser known factories are known now only because of deeds, documents, stock certificates, and a few pieces owned by descendants of workmen or investors. Only recently the writers found a piece of pressed glass marked Pioneer Flint Glass Co., Coffeyville, Kansas. Since none of the current volumes had any data on this factory, research was started on the spot, with the assistance of the local postmaster and the chamber of commerce. Coffeyville made pressed glass for the surrounding area in the early 1900s. Certain far western-owned pressed glass, in as yet unnamed "patterns," may turn out to be Coffeyville pressed glass.

Pressed glass, beyond the classic rarities of Sandwich and lacy Sandwich, is a product that covered the country like a blanket. No other common things, with the exception of buttons, match covers, and postage stamps, were made in quantities comparable to pressed glass. It was the cheapest glassware ever made in world history. It was sold in cheap stores from 1850 onward to the

SANDWICH CUP PLATES

EARLY JERSEY GLASS

days of Woolworth and Sears, Roebuck. Its final phase
was a direct imitation of the deep-cut heavy crystal that
was considered good taste at the turn of the twentieth
century. Any phase of pressed-glass production prior to
that period holds great charm for many collectors. "Sets
in pattern" is one collector's vagary. Milk glass in many
varieties is another vagary. One could, if one wished, fill
a book just with entries of what any odd three thousand
pressed-glass collectors fancy as their current quest.
Most of this ware was made in Pennsylvania, but some
of it came out of West Virginia, Massachusetts, and
Ohio.

One of the important collecting pursuits today has to
do with historic bottles and flasks. These were made in
tremendous quantities, mostly as containers for whisky.
It should be remembered that when these bottles
achieved popularity, whisky was an untaxed beverage
sold everywhere, even in grocery stores. The price was
low; some of it sold for $1.00 a gallon. Buying a half
pint, a pint, or a quart was an everyday occurrence. It
was seldom, if ever, sold bottled by the distiller. It was
sold by the barrel and dispensed from the barrel—into
bottles supplied by the vendor. Usually the bottles were
of the flat oval type, blown with designs, such as busts,
emblems, and other insignia.

Almost every glass factory made such bottles, not in
one design but in anywhere from one to fifty designs
and in varieties of sizes, shapes, and colors. Important
men, historically and otherwise, were memorialized;
political candidates were promoted; all kinds of public
works, trades, and pursuits were given attention by the
bottle designers. That most of these bottles came from
the Pittsburgh-Wheeling-Allegheny region is now generally known, but they were also made in tremendous
quantities at Philadelphia, Baltimore, and at various

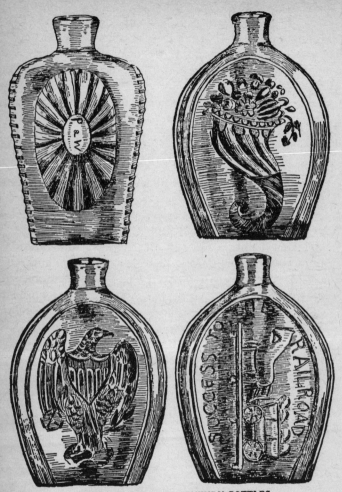

EARLY NINETEENTH-CENTURY BOTTLES

glass factories in New Hampshire, Massachusetts, Connecticut, New York, and Ohio. It can be said without stretching the truth one bit that these bottles were made almost everywhere that glass was made, and used everywhere in these United States.

There has been some question as to the source of the idea for the blown molded bottle. One New York dealer has such a bottle of early production marked, and identifiable, as the product of a Swedish glass furnace of about 1820. It is believed that imports of liquor in such bottles fell into the hands of glass manufacturers who saw in the idea a splendid way of developing a new business. They made the bottles and enjoyed a volume of business that may well have totaled several million bottles a year.

One most interesting thing in connection with glass collecting is that many of these historic flasks are marked with the name of the maker, or the glass factory, or the place of manufacture—and sometimes all three of these important data. This is to say that the most accurately identifiable glass produced in America resides in the production of historic glass.

Chapter XVIII

POTTERY AND PORCELAIN

FEW seventeenth-century records dealing with early colonial production of earthenware or redware pottery have been preserved. Perhaps so commonplace a thing as a potter's kiln was considered unworthy of comment. From what records we do have we can be sure that ordinary red pottery, glazed and unglazed, was made at Jamestown after 1610 and that before 1650 several potters were in Virginia making simple earthenware for household use. We can also be sure that wherever bricks were made, some common redwares were made and fired in the brick kilns. In addition to bricks and potwork, some of these kilns also produced roofing tiles.

Brickmaking seems to have been well established in Virginia and New England by 1647. In Pennsylvania brickyards of considerable size are commented upon as in operation by 1685. The wares made at these yards and in small potteries were in imitation of the currently popular output of common wares in the Staffordshire district of England. Milk pans, char pots, dishes, griddles, mugs, jugs, and jars were made in Staffordshire and most likely made in the colonies. These cheap wares were seldom decorated. When decorated, however, the decoration was in the very same types of crude figures, animalistic representations, and tulips which are found on the redwares of Massachusetts, New York, Pennsylvania, Maryland, and Virginia. All of these colonial wares seem to follow the Staffordshire tradition in shape, form, and decoration. In Pennsylvania, and in the Shenandoah Valley, some Swiss decorative forms, in addition to Staffordshire, were introduced. These are not unlike the forms used by the Staffordshire potters of the seventeenth century. The Dutch, in their efforts to imitate the porcelains from the Orient then commonly called "china," used a tin glaze on redware. This pottery, decorated somewhat in the Chinese manner and with blue pigment, was called Delftware. Pottery of similar nature was made in the Dutch colony on the Hudson and perhaps in the Hoarkill Valley of what was later Pennsylvania. In 1735 Remmey was making stoneware in New York. The first stoneware made in the colonies seems to have been made in New Jersey, where a pottery for its production was set up in 1684-88 by Daniel Cox of London. This pottery was in the vicinity of Burlington.

Stoneware is a hard-bodied pottery which, in spite of its crudity, is a first cousin of the fine porcelains of China. Redware is soft-bodied pottery. In Pennsylvania, and in the New York and New England colonies, a form of redware decoration known as sgraffito was sometimes practiced. This technique is quite simple. A piece of dried but unfired redware is coated with a thin layer of white clay. This is permitted to dry on the red clay body. Then the design or decoration is scratched through the white clay coating down to the red clay. When fired and glazed, the design shows up in red on the white surface. Sometimes mottling of green was added before firing and hence the ware has the appearance of three-colored decoration. The other method of decorating redware is a modification of sgraffito that sounds simpler but isn't. White clay is thinned to the consistency of cream and placed in a cup from which quills convey it to a writing or drawing point. This contrivance, a sort of crude fountain pen, held in the hand of the decorator, was used to trace designs on the redware. Dots, lines, lettering, curlicues, and other decoration were thus put on the red clay body. When a double or triple line was desired, two and three quills were used. That's how the multiple wavy lines sometimes found on redwares were applied. We have tried both methods of decorating, working for some days in an old pottery. We found sgraffito the simplest and most satisfactory method of decorating yet, somehow, this is apparently the method least used by our early potters. Sgraffito techniques were used by the potters of England, the Netherlands, and Switzerland for almost the same types of pottery our American potters selected for its application: presentation and ceremonial pieces. These objects were usually for show and not for general household use. The same thing is true of elaborately made pieces with slip decoration. They were the fancy things, usually bespoke, or made to order, and not produced as general items for sale.

Many names of late redware potters have been culled from the tax rolls of various communities in all of the states covered in this *New Geography of American Antiques*. Most of these potters were working between 1785 and 1865. Up to as late as 1930 it was generally supposed that all slip and sgraffito decorated redwares were of Pennsylvania origin. We now know that all the states had redware potters using the same techniques once erroneously thought to be the mark of Pennsylvania ware.

Before considering certain of the outstanding potters and porcelain makers who produced wares in our country it might be well to deal with the generally accepted definitions of various pottery terms. *China*, or *china-ware*, was the generic name given to the porcelains of

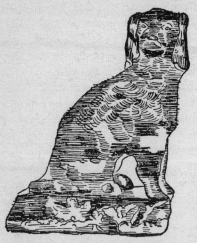

BLUE POTTERY DOG FROM
NEW JERSEY

EARLY PENNSYLVANIA PLATE WITH FIGURE
DECORATION

China when they were imported to Europe. Almost at once Italian and Dutch potters attempted to imitate this mysterious ware. They developed *majolica* and *delft*. But these were not true porcelains and therefore not true chinaware. The secret of Chinese porcelain was discovered by a German alchemist when attempting to make hard crucibles in which he planned to transmute base metals into gold. Within a short while the secret was discovered by others, but to the early ware known as *Meissen*, or *Dresden*, must go the palm of honor for the first duplication of true Chinese ware. English potters did not hit upon the precise secret but they did develop a ware which the Chinese might have envied. This was "bone china," not called bone because it was hard but because calcined bones were a part of the clay mixture used in its making.

The stonewares of Europe and England were the closest approximation to Chinese porcelains before the discovery of the porcelain secret. This secret was the use of kaolin clay and feldspar which, fused in firing the clay, produced a very hard, glass-like body. For the purpose of quick differentiation, pottery is divided into two classes—*hard paste* and *soft paste*. Another class, *semi-hard*, stands between, just to make the difference a bit confusing. Chinese and other true porcelains and stonewares are hard paste. English bone china, redwares, slipwares, delft, majolica, and all other earthenwares are soft paste. Of course every definition in the field of pottery can be questioned as to strict veracity. For example, to say "all earthenwares are soft paste" isn't true at all. Hard-paste porcelains are also made of earth; hence they are earthenwares. So what is meant is that all earthenwares other than kaolin-feldspar wares are soft paste. English bone china stands, actually, half-way between soft and hard paste. From the standpoint of service in use this ware is perhaps more satisfactory than either hard or soft paste. It is the happy medium in fine pottery.

Even the terms hard paste and soft paste are misleading to the uninitiated. Both types of pottery, in the paste form, are equally soft and plastic. Both, in the biscuit or first-fired form, are quite "hard" to the touch. What is really meant by hard paste and soft paste is this: a rat-tail file will gouge into the fired clay of soft paste but will be "turned" by the fired clay of hard paste. Soft pastes, generally, are opaque while true porcelain is translucent, but there are unglazed red porcelains that are not translucent and there are some bone chinas having certain qualities of translucence.

Abraham and Andrew Miller succeeded to the Philadelphia pottery established by their father in 1790. Abraham Miller is supposed to have made the first silver lusterware in this country. He produced a great variety of pottery, including Rockingham "Tam O' Shanter" mugs and decorated tableware. Miller experimented with hard-paste porcelain but never manufactured it for commerical purposes.

William Ellis Tucker, son of Benjamin Tucker, a Quaker, opened a china shop in Philadelphia and experimented in decorating imported white china which he fired in a small kiln constructed by his father. Later Tucker made simple pottery and experimented in producing hard-paste porcelain. After many failures he succeeded in producing a good quality porcelain. In 1826 Tucker built a factory at Philadelphia. In 1827 he was awarded a medal by the Franklin Institute for the best gold-decorated porcelain made in Pennsylvania. The workmanship of this piece was poor, but the paste and glaze were of unusual quality. In 1828 he received a medal for the best porcelain made in the United States, and this time the workmanship was of much better type. The name of his firm was now Tucker & Hulme. In 1829 Hulme withdrew and Tucker continued alone until 1832, when he formed a partnership with Joseph Hemphill. Soon after this Tucker died and his place in the firm was taken by Robert C. Hemphill. Thomas Tucker, his son, was retained as superintendent of the works. The Tucker factory reproduced with considerable skill the decorative designs used by the Sèvres factory in France. Much of the Tucker ware was left unmarked because of the current feeling throughout this country that the best of everything should be imported and never locally made.

The Jersey Porcelain & Earthenware Company began operations in 1825 at Jersey City. This firm produced common yellow and white wares and gold-decorated porcelain of excellent quality. After three years of manufacture, porcelain production was discontinued. In 1835 the company name was changed to The American Pottery Company. One of the novelties manufactured then was a hound-handle pitcher, the sides of which bore hunting scenes in relief. The handle represented a crouching hound with his nose on the rim of the top. This was an adaptation of a favorite English model, designed by Daniel Greatback, who came here from England in 1836. In 1839 the English transfer printing process was introduced and used by this pottery in the production of tablewares.

For many years pottery clay from South Amboy, New Jersey, was shipped to kilns in other sections of the country. It was not until 1807 that Warne and Letts opened the first pottery in South Amboy. They marked their wares, which is the only way we can tell them from the pottery of John Hancock. Hancock came from England and in 1810 opened a factory at South Amboy, devoted to the manufacture of yellow ware and stoneware.

That Holland was interested in establishing a pottery in New Amsterdam at an early date was shown by the fact that the Dutch East India Trading Company in 1645 sent Jan Van Arsdale to New Amsterdam to ascertain whether it was practicable to establish a pottery in the new country. A pottery seems to have been built about 1646–48, but no records exist to give information concerning its output.

Very little fine pottery was produced in New England before the Revolution. What was made was of simple design to serve utilitarian needs. After the colonies became free there was a greater incentive to manufacture for home consumption and a number of small potteries sprang up. Many of the potters were engaged in other professions and turned only their spare moments to the making of a few dishes and jars. The first kilns used did not involve any great expenditure of money but turned out an amazing variety of household utensils. Pieces from early kilns were of lead-glazed red clay with some slip decoration. In nearly every known instance they were unsigned. Salt-glazed stonewares were made in considerable quantity and these wares, in most cases, bore the signature of their maker. Nearly all New England pottery of early date shows an unmistakable English influence, good color and glaze.

In 1785 Captain John Norton moved with his family from Connecticut to Bennington, Vermont, to undertake farming on a small scale. In 1793 he laid the foundation of a pottery on his farm at Old Bennington. There was great need for simple household utensils in the nearby

HOUND-HANDLE PITCHER

STONEWARE JUG

CONNECTICUT STONEWARE WITH DECORATED AND SCRATCHED
EMBELLISHMENTS

homes. Norton at first made only common types of earth-enware—plates, platters, jugs, and jars. Before 1800 he began making stoneware at his pottery. In 1823 he retired from active business. His sons, Luman and John, succeeded him. Until the dissolution of the firm in 1828 the stoneware of this pottery was marked "Norton & Company." This is supposed to have been the first mark used by the Norton potteries.

A new and larger pottery was built in 1833 at East Bennington by Luman Norton and his son Julius who, in 1841, held entire control of the works. Apparently he was not satisfied to make red clay and stoneware only and began the manufacture of yellow ware and Rockingham. The latter is the yellow ware spattered with brown clay before it is fired, to give a mottled appearance.

In 1844 the firm of Norton & Fenton was formed. Christopher Webber Fenton had operated a pottery at Dorset, Vermont, before coming to Bennington. The stoneware and Rockingham pieces made during this period were signed "Norton & Fenton, East Bennington, Vermont," "Norton & Fenton, Bennington, Vermont," or sometimes just "Norton & Fenton."

With the closing of the Hemphill works in Philadelphia in 1837 the making of soft paste porcelain was discontinued in this country. In 1843 it was revived at Bennington, and for a few years was made in small quantities. In 1845 the factory burned and it was not until two years later that the manufacture of porcelain could be resumed. Much of this ware was of uneven quality and without glazing. Kaolin and feldspar were both found near at hand in large quantities. Parian wares in the form of statues and vases were made as early as 1842. Norton & Fenton Parian was an especially prepared hard-paste unglazed porcelain which resembled marble

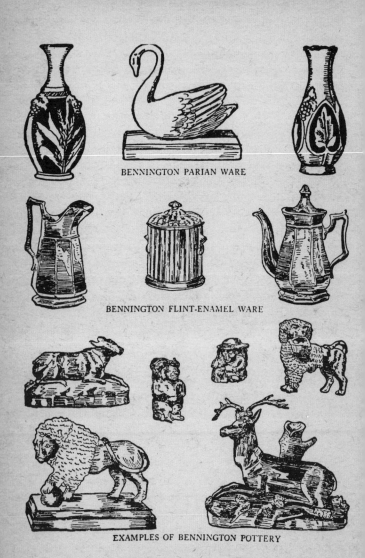

BENNINGTON PARIAN WARE

BENNINGTON FLINT-ENAMEL WARE

EXAMPLES OF BENNINGTON POTTERY

in texture. For its decorative pieces it was admirable, but it was almost worthless for household wares.

In 1849 Fenton obtained from the United States Government a patent for the process of applying colors to enamel wares. This Fenton flint enamel was a mottling of yellow and olive-green, yellow and black, yellow, brown, green, dark red, and a very little blue.

The hound-handle pitcher designed for the Bennington pottery by Daniel Greatback differed only slightly from the one he modeled for the Jersey City pottery. In the Bennington pitcher the nose of the hound is not so near the top edge of the rim and slight variations appear in the dog collar. The actual ware was much finer and generally brown, although it was sometimes made in green or blue glaze. The branch-handle and tulip-design pitchers are unusually charming and much sought after today. The cow creamer, lion with its paw on a ball, the coachman and deer are all well-known designs of Greatback. The common poodle with a basket in his mouth seems to have been designed by some other modeler.

The fact that pottery molds were often made by firms who sold to any potter wanting to buy them makes it very hard to distinguish and classify unmarked pieces of American pottery. As workers left one factory and went to another, they carried into their new work certain characteristics of the old, with the result that styles and methods became so intermingled that it is practically impossible for us to determine exact origins. Occasionally when a firm discontinued business the machinery and molds were sold to another firm, with similar results. This happened in the case of Abraham Miller, who purchased the equipment used by Hemphill when Thomas Tucker closed the business. The potter's wheel was used in some manufactories and in most small redware pot-

TUCKER CHINA

teries, but large producers depended upon plaster-of-Paris molds for continuous production and duplication of their items.

There were many small potteries making simple red-wares in the new state of Ohio before the Englishman, James Bennett, set up a pottery at East Liverpool in 1840 for the production of red pottery and Rockingham ware. There are extant a number of engaging items in stoneware from small Ohio potteries, some of them, either bespoke or workman's pieces, having molded, applied, and incised decoration. The clay deposits of Ohio and the tremendous demand for potted wares from the westward quite naturally fostered the development of a potting industry in this state. In the early days the Allegheny Mountains were a considerable barrier to commerce. Eastern potteries couldn't supply the Western states and territories. Ohio, with the lakes as a waterway to its north, with navigable streams flowing both north and south, and with the Ohio River open to sea and tapping the vast Ohio-Mississippi Valley, was a natural producing ground. As with furniture, so with pottery, is the history of Ohio production. Soon redwares were but a small part of the pottery manufacture. China-making factories were started, thrived and prospered. The one famous American art pottery, Rookwood, is made at Cincinnati, Ohio. Rookwood, of course, is not in any sense antique, but early and late Rookwood is nonetheless much sought after by advanced collectors and almost every museum in the land is glad to have examples of it on display.

Late production of majolica wares from Pennsylvania, some of it sold as late as 1890 in cheap stores, is today collected by many people. It is not for us to chide these collectors. They are buying up items destined one day to be valuable and they are doing, in their own way,

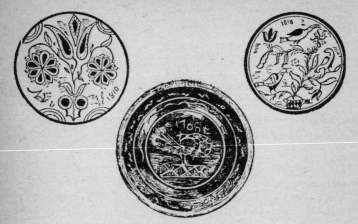

EARLY PENNSYLVANIA PLATES OF SGRAFFIATO

POTTERY EAGLE FROM PHŒNIXVILLE,
PENNSYLVANIA

precisely what the late Edwin Atlee Barber of Philadelphia did fifty years ago. He began collecting Pennsylvania slipwares. Some of the wares he then collected were little more than sixty years old. Today they are almost priceless possessions of the Philadelphia Museum.

Chapter XIX

PEWTER AND SILVER

PEWTER is an alloy of tin with copper and lead or antimony. The greater the amount of tin used the more silvery the pewter appears. In fine pewter the tin content runs as high as 90 per cent. The poorer grades of pewter reveal less than 60 per cent of tin. An excess of lead gives pewter a dark, dull look and a softness that is objectionable because the ware dents quite easily.

Good pewter is smooth to the touch and has a peculiarly lovely tone—something between silver and burnished steel—and can be polished to a subdued luster that is quite different from other metals. Pewter was used by the Chinese more than two thousand years ago. The Romans used a form of pewter for their official seals. They procured tin from the mines of Albion—from England. France and England used pewter in the eleventh century. The alloy was in quite general use in most European countries in the fifteenth century.

Our early settlers brought very little pewter with them but soon voiced their need for it. Among the first things asked for from the mother country were pewter bottles—bottles that did not break. During the seventeenth and eighteenth centuries the colonists used a great deal of pewter. Even the wealthy did not always have silver and fine china suitable for everyday use. Between the years 1750 and 1770 much pewter was made, but along with lead clock weights a great deal of it went into the melting pot during the Revolutionary War.

For everyday household wares pewter has long since been replaced with harder white metals, nickel and plated silver. Most of the early pewter was imported from Europe with Boston, New York, and Philadelphia as the distributing centers. There is a record, however, of one pewterer working in Boston in the 1640s, some years before we find mention of the first silversmith. It was not long before other pewterers arrived and set up shops in various towns. Being well trained, for the most part, our early pewterers turned out splendid work. Possibly they had less variety in patterns than their fellow craftsmen across the ocean, yet their work suited the local demand and could readily be fashioned to suit the choice of the individual purchaser.

There were three methods of making pewter: hammering by hand, spinning, and casting in molds. At times a combination of two or even all three of these methods was used. The finishing, in general, was done carefully by hand, but a lathe was often also used.

England as well as France shipped fine china and pottery to the colonies. This went into the better-class homes where it replaced pewter, perhaps by 1765. Pewter candlesticks, cans, whale-oil lamps, and similar objects were made until the latter half of the nineteenth century. It would seem that the trade of the pewterer was not a very lucrative one, for in many cases we find it combined with other forms of business such as blacksmithing, clockmaking, and eventually even plumbing!

The average size of plates was eight inches, although they varied from six and a quarter to twenty inches. This latter size was exceptional. Thirteen inches was ordinarily the largest size. Mixing bowls and serving dishes were from six and a half inches in diameter to the rare twelve-

EXAMPLES OF EARLY SILVERWARE

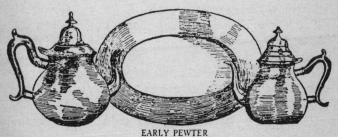

EARLY PEWTER

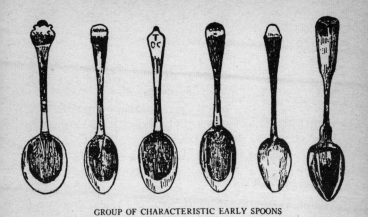

GROUP OF CHARACTERISTIC EARLY SPOONS

EXAMPLES OF EARLY SILVERWARE

inch ones. By 1825 china had almost entirely replaced pewter as a tableware. A feeling of prosperity had swept in and better and more fashionable household things were in demand.

Early American pewter marks, though not typically English, showed a strong English influence. After the Revolutionary War the marks became more individual in style. In Massachusetts and Rhode Island the state coat of arms was used at times. About 1790 the American eagle was used as a mark by some pewterers. After the first quarter of the nineteenth century pewter marks lost individuality and became more standardized, often the name or name and address of the maker was used as an identification stamp.

One of the earliest colonial pewterers was Thomas Danforth, who lived from 1703 to 1786. His output varied from tea and coffee pots to lamps and candlesticks, in addition to all kinds of flatwares and porringers. He worked at Taunton, Massachusetts, and at Norwich, Connecticut. His pieces show skilled craftsmanship and are treasured by collectors. Boston had Nathaniel Austen, who was famous in his trade in the latter half of the eighteenth century and who produced many fine examples of this metalware. In 1743 John Holden of New York advertised his wares, pewter utensils, hollow and flatware. His shop was in Market Slip. Francis Basset, whose name is found in the 1786 directory of New York, was listed as a pewterer. At that time there were in New York Robert Byle, William Bradford, Henry Will, and Malcolm McEwen, each of whose pewter deserves consideration. The Philadelphia City Directory of 1785 boasted of Colonel William Will as the outstanding pewterer of the city.

Lancaster, Pennsylvania, boasts its John Christopher Heyne who made pewter c. 1750 to 1780. His ware is

Benj. Burt

John Burt

perhaps the rarest of all American pewter. "J.C.H. Lancaster" on a piece of pewter is the mark that makes Heyne pewter more valuable than silver.

As we study trade history in the second quarter of the nineteenth century the pewterers seem to disappear from the scene. Most of them either became plumbers or, if they kept shop, sold the new Britannia ware. This ware found a splendid mass market which willingly forgot about pewter and pewter makers.

It is perhaps natural that the Southern colonies with large plantations, whose owners held to the customs and traditions of the mother country, were the first to boast ownership of any great amount of silver. The wealthier life, to which many of the Southern settlers had been accustomed, included all of the so-called luxuries. In coming to this new country they changed residence but not their philosophy of life. A considerable amount of English plate was used in Virginia and the Carolinas. Standish Barry of Baltimore was one of the best known early Southern silversmiths. He followed English design but his craftsmanship did not equal that of his contemporaries in New York or Boston.

Seventeenth-century Boston was a major commercial center of the colonies. Considerable sums of money, especially Spanish silver coin, found their way to this port. The absence of banking facilities and the fluctuation of the English shilling created a desire on the part of the colonists to convert their surplus silver into articles suitable for domestic use. This gave to the silversmiths of Boston an unusual volume of business for that day and age.

The silversmiths of colonial days were not only skilled craftsmen but usually took an active part in church and civic affairs and were held in high esteem by their fellowmen. The first silversmith of prominence in Boston was

PEWTER SHIP'S LIGHT

JOHN CONEY

John Hull, who came from England in 1635. Because of the scarcity of English currency for local trade, the General Court of Massachusetts in 1652, in defiance of the Crown, decided to coin shillings and fractions thereof. These were the famed "pine-tree" shillings which weighed three pennyweight. The die for this coin was made by Joseph Jenks of Lynn, Massachusetts. Hull was appointed mint master and for his services received one shilling out of every twenty. He was also financially interested in trade with the West Indies, acquired a large fortune, and was very active in public affairs. He had a partner, Robert Sanderson, and continued in business until his death in 1683. Some fine early silver still exists marked with the names of these two men.

Jeremiah Dummer (1645–1718) was apprenticed to Hull and acquired much of the technique of his master. One of the distinctive forms of decoration used frequently by Dummer is the fluted band. This appears to advantage on tankards and standing cups. Dummer's brother-in-law, John Cony (1655–1722), also became a leading silversmith and engraver. He made the plates for the first paper money issued in the American colonies. Edward Winslow (1669–1753) produced silver of such fine quality as to rank him one, if not the greatest, of the earlier craftsmen.

Later came the Reveres, father and son, Apollus Revoir (1702–54) was born in France and came to Boston in 1715. He served his apprenticeship under John Cony. In 1723 he started in business for himself and changed his name to Paul Revere. His son Paul (1735–1818) was the third oldest of twelve children. He learned the craft from his father, who taught him silversmithing and engraving. Young Paul Revere was only nineteen when his father died. He at once started conducting shop. The

EXAMPLES OF EARLY SILVERWARE

PAUL REVERE TEA URN AND TEAPOTS

plate for our national paper currency was engraved by Paul Revere in 1775.

Newport was the center of the silversmith's art in Rhode Island. Samuel Vernon (1683–1737) was the first maker of note. Later, in Providence, Jabez Gorham laid the foundation of a business which his descendants have carried on.

Connecticut, being an agricultural colony, could not boast of great wealth. The silversmiths of this colony frequently followed several lines of business. Much of the silver owned by Connecticut churches was made in Boston or New York. Cornelius Kierstede from New York settled at New Haven about 1722. He was a skillful silversmith whose work shows a blending of Dutch and English influence.

Conditions in the New Netherlands were quite different from those in New England as far the the silversmithing craft was concerned. The Dutch established settlements primarily as trading posts and although they soon learned colonization was necessary, they did very little to assist the early settlers. It was not until 1650 that the colony began to increase to any extent. Trading had been carried on through the Dutch West India Company, exchanging furs and raw materials for the manufactured goods of Holland. The wealthy usually imported most, if not all, of their luxuries. When the English acquired New Netherlands from the Dutch in 1664, New Amsterdam had a population of less than thirty-five hundred. Although the name was changed to New York, Dutch customs and traditions prevailed, as was clearly shown in the silver made there. New York's seventeenth-century silver is purely Dutch in design. By the middle of the eighteenth century we find the English influence prevailing. The early pieces were simple in design and beautifully executed, with a considerable

amount of engraving and ornamentation. The shape and
design were always appropriate to the metal used and
to the use for which the piece was intended. The pieces
were more massive and the silver thicker than those of
New England, but there was less refinement of line and
artistic finish.

One of the earliest of New Amsterdam's silversmiths
was Jacob Boelin (1654–1729), who came from Holland
to New Amsterdam about 1659. Peter Van Dyke, with
his wonderful genius, was considered one of the finest
silversmiths of colonial times. He was born in New York
in 1684 and was actively interested in political affairs.
His son Richard was also a craftsman of note. About
1690 a number of French Protestants, seeking refuge
from religious persecution, settled in New York; among
them were skillful silversmiths such as Bartholomew le
Roux, the father-in-law of Peter Van Dyke. These men
introduced a certain amount of French design and
technique into the work they did in the colony.

Pennsylvania, under the able leadership of William
Penn, was prosperous from the start. Philadelphia soon
became an important commercial center and, until well
into the nineteenth century, was the largest city in the
country. The silversmiths were offered ample opportunity
to display their skill. Pennsylvania silver differs very little in design from that produced in other English colonies. The alms basin made for Christ's Church, Philadelphia, is the work of Cesar Chieselin, one of the first
silversmiths. He was a Huguenot, going first to England
and finally coming to Philadelphia, where he died about
1733. Philip Syng (1676–1739) was another silversmith
of note. His son, Philip Syng, Jr. (1703–89), made the
inkstand used when the Declaration of Independence
was signed. As early as 1740 Daniel Syng was making

PAUL REVERE

silverware at Lancaster. By 1785 almost every Pennsylvania town had its quota of silversmiths.

Pure silver, because of its softness, was alloyed with other metals, especially copper, to harden it. Most early silver was made from coins which, melted and refined to the desired standard, were thus taken out of circulation. The colonies had no legally established silver standard as did England; the early silversmiths were considered honorable men and their name or mark stamped on a piece was accepted as sufficient evidence of quality. Their method of attaining a desired standard was to rub a piece of their own silver on a touchstone and compare the color of touch with that made by silver of known quality and fineness.

Silver metal was melted and poured into shallow rectangular pans. When these cast pieces were cold they were rolled or hammered into sheets of the thickness required. The more silver is hammered the harder and more brittle it becomes so, to prevent it from cracking, it was necessary to heat the work from time to time by means of a charcoal fire. The peculiar bluish-gray tint almost always found in old silver came from oxygen in the air and the copper in the alloy which combined when heated in the furnaces of the smiths. We do not find this copper oxide on present-day silver; modern methods of making remove it entirely. In making hollowware, silver was rolled into thin sheets and beaten into desired shapes with a mallet of wood or metal on blocks or anvils. After this shaping, surface decorations in the form of engraving, chasing, piercing or repoussé work were added.

Beakers or tall cups were among the earliest pieces of silver made in the colonies. These were made both for church and domestic use. They were usually engraved with symbolic figures, floral scrolls or festoons, and had a strong molding at the base. At the time of the Reformation, the chalice was replaced by the beaker in the Protestant churches of Holland. Naturally the Dutch colonists followed this custom in New Netherlands. This accounts for the many beakers found that were used in the churches of New York. In New England, in addition to beakers, churches used tankards, chalices, and caudle cups in the communion services.

The beaker of New Netherlands was about seven inches tall. It flared slightly at the top and tapered toward the flat bottom. There was a heavy torus molding at the base, above which was a cutwork foliate border, a spiral wire, or an ornamental band. The lip was usually engraved in designs using scrolls, strapwork, and sometimes medallions. The early type of New England beaker was smaller and plainer, with straight sides and a flat bottom generally without molding. Later examples were taller, still plain, but with a molding on the base. The straight-side beakers were followed by others with slightly bulbous sides; later came the style of straight sides with molded bands at top and base.

The tankard of the seventeenth century had a slightly tapering body, broad flat base, flat-hinged lid, and heavy handle. Those made by the New Netherlands silversmiths were of generous proportions, almost always cylindrical in shape. The flat lid was usually embossed or engraved, the handles ornamented and tipped with designs more or less elaborate. The foliage border above the base molding and corkscrew thumbpiece were very characteristic. The New England type of tankard, up to the first part of the eighteenth century, was comparatively low and broad and had a flat lid; later New England tankards had domed lids with simply designed finials added. The flame and pine cone were popular finial motifs.

It was not until after 1700 that colonial silversmiths made tea, coffee, and chocolate pots. Originally all of these were small, the beverages being too expensive to use in quantity. During the eighteenth century tea, coffee, and chocolate became cheaper and the size of the pots in which to brew and serve them increased accordingly. In general outline, tea and coffee pots were similar but in size the coffeepot was the larger. Chocolate pots had straighter spouts with the handle at right angles to it, a tapering body, and high domed lid. A small hole in the lid usually marked the chocolate pot. This hole was for the swizzle, or rotary stirring rod, used to whip the chocolate beverage when making and serving it. Early eighteenth-century New England teapots were of two types—one round, with flat lid and splayed molded base, "S"-shaped spout, and "C"-shaped wooden handle, and the other bell-shaped, with domed lid, the base flat with a small molding, short "S"-shaped spout, and curved wooden handle with thumbpiece.

The New York teapots were somewhat different in appearance—the lower part of the bulbous body being flatter and the neck narrowed and longer. Molded bands defined the contour of the body and the domed lid. Engraving on the body and the spiral wire and pattern border at the base are typical.

By the middle of the eighteenth century we find the shapes changed: the body of the teapot resembles an inverted pear. There is a slight "S" curve in the decorated spout, which projects well away from the body. The foot is molded and splayed and the lid small, slightly rounded, and topped by a finial. The decorations by this time were showing less of the rococo influence that marks the so-called Chippendale period silver and were more classical in feeling. Bands of reeding and beaded moldings, engraved festoons of flowers, rosettes, oval

PAUL REVERE

medallions, and "bright-cut" designs were popular. The oval-shaped teapots had straight or slightly curved sides and there was no molding around the top or the flat base. Often there was a small tray with feet for the pot to rest upon. The spout was straight and the lid was either flat, slightly belled, or concave with a finial of silver, ivory, wood, or bone.

During the early part of the nineteenth century French influence is apparent in our silverware designs, particularly in our hollow wares. The pieces were of thinner silver, larger in size, and many were on ball feet. About 1800 a pierced railing on the tea and coffee pots and also sugar bowls marks the silver of Philadelphia make.

Porringers seem to have been among the most popular and hence useful pieces of household silverware. They were used for both solid and liquid food, for sauces and tidbits. Most of them are between five and six inches in diameter, about two inches deep, with a flat handle set nearly flush with the rim. These handles afforded silversmiths opportunity to display their designing ability. Flat openwork designs of geometric or "keyhole" character mark most silver porringer handles.

Forks were scarce in early colonial days but became quite common in the eighteenth century. Some were all silver and others had silver handles only, with prongs or tines of steel. The handles were usually of the same shape and design as the spoons. Sauceboats, creamers, salt cellars, and braziers of the eighteenth century were generally set on three legs, which ended in a scroll or hoof.

Spoons are probably the earliest of the domestic utensils. During the seventeenth century the spoon had undergone several changes, so by 1660 we find the bowl becoming more oval than round, the stem flatter and thinner, with a notched or trifid end. The bowl and stem were joined by a long plain tongue, often called a "rattail," which was frequently bordered by a design. In the eighteenth century the end of the handle was rounded and turned in the same direction as the bowl. There was a sharp ridge on the front of the rounded stem near the end. Following the rattail there was the double drop on the bowl. Then the end of the stem was turned down and the ridge became very faint. The double drop on the bowl was superseded by the single drop, and such ornaments as a scroll, bird, and shell. The fiddle handle was popular about 1810. The bowl had a pointed tip and there was a broad shoulder above the bowl and the stem where it widens.

After 1790 silversmiths flourished everywhere within our federal boundaries. By 1850 many "jewelers and silversmiths" had ceased to make silver but sold the mass-produced sterling or coin silver of other makers who had started factories. In this these merchants were doing precisely what Paul Revere did after the Revolution. It is a matter of record in many sections of the country that rural and small-town silversmiths made spoons, forks, creamers, and other items in considerable quantities which they sold, either unmarked or marked with the stamp of the jewelry-store customer with whom they had contracted for production. Between 1800 and 1850 about half of the clockmakers appears to have dabbled in silversmithing and many of them actually did very presentable work. There was hardly a city or town of any consequence in the early federal era that did not boast having anywhere from one to a dozen silversmiths. Some of these men turned out delightful "local" patterns, or variants of popular patterns. At Bethlehem, Pennsylvania, one silversmith marked the bottom of his teaspoons with a large spread eagle at the point of juncture with the handle. This was not his identification mark; he marked the silver with his name. In his own way he conceived of making silver patriotic and of having the national emblem on every spoon he made.

The records of nineteenth-century silversmiths and the listing of the men at work have been neglected phases of American silversmith history up to comparatively recent times. Since 1930 an effort has been made to tabulate all of the nineteenth-century men working up to 1850. This work, by Stephen G. C. Ensko, is now on press and, it is hoped, will soon be generally available to students and collectors. It is probable that as many men were working at silversmithing between 1800 and 1850 as there were silversmiths working in all the years from 1660 to 1800. This bespeaks a tremendous production of American silver. There is no valid reason, aesthetic or otherwise, why silverware of the first half of the nineteenth century should not be collected. We have just focused all our attention on the very early silver that is now almost priceless; we have glorified the silver of Revere and other famous makers for purely emotional reasons; and we have collected early federal-era silver in the fond belief that it was colonial. The silverware of the rococo period—or the Chippendale era—between the years 1765 and 1785 has never been very popular with any of the seasoned collectors. It is too, too fussy— in fact, some of it is fusty. The decoration is overloaded —a caricature of what it could have been had the decoration been used with taste and restraint.

One phenomenon apparent in our silver, as it is in our furniture production, deserves mention here. Back-country silversmiths continued to make silver in styles of periods no longer popular in large and sophisticated communities. Charles Hall, of Lancaster, Pennsylvania, was making silver in the Queen Anne style up to 1776.

Other silversmiths at or near the frontiers of any colony were doing the same thing. This is why so much silverware made in small towns, or almost any silverware made out of the large cities from 1800 to 1825, is apt to reflect styles that were the vogue in the 1790s. That, also, is why we should pay more attention to early nineteenth-century silver. It is really worthy of serious collecting.

Chapter XX

FLOOR COVERINGS, COVERLETS, AND TEXTILES

THE first fine floor covering used in our colonial homes was a heavy painted floorcloth displaying tessellated or tile-like patterns. In a few words, this was the great-great-grandfather of today's inlaid linoleum: sailcloth, coated over and over with filler, laid out in diamonds or squares, and painted in contrasting blocks of colors! Sometimes the blocks of color were plain, sometimes marbleized, and sometimes treated as areas for individual decoration. Such cloths were made to cover the entire wood floor from baseboard to baseboard. When this could not be afforded, pieces were used under and around the tables—especially dining tables.

Floors were sanded before the floorcloth was available. That is, the floor was covered with an inch or so of fine white sand, often "raked and brushed" into a design not unlike cake frosting. The minute such a design was stepped on it was mussed. But, even so, the sand protected wood floors from mud, grease, and droppings. Also it sealed cracks and prevented drafts at baseboard joints.

Before the pioneers' wood floors, whether bare, sanded, or covered with a painted floorcloth, the floor was earth covered with rushes and reeds. These were the floors of the first cottages and cabins. They often turned into a miniature bog in protracted wet weather.

Because the painted floorcloth, certainly by 1700, had

259

captured the imagination of all colonists who could afford it, these luxury items were imported as a regular thing. Almost every important portrait painted after 1675 which displays a section of floor, displays what many heretofore have thought was artistic license—a floor of marble tiles. But this was not artists' license—it is a picture of the cloth that was on the floor. No matter how amazing it may sound, a floor of modern inlaid linoleum, in black-and-white squares, can be laid on the floor of any house built after 1675, and the floor scheme will be in perfect period and pattern!

Those who could not afford the painted floorcloth found a quick substitute in painting the floor in imitation of the floorcloth. So popular was this fashion that itinerant floor painters peddled their services in cities, towns, villages, and along country lanes.

It was over the painted floorcloth and over the painted floors that rugs and carpets, when available, were laid. Many quite early inventories mention rugs and carpets but these, again amazingly, were not for the floors. They were bedcoverings, table covers, chimney cloths, and window-sill covers. Not unless an inventory specifically mentions the carpet as for a bedside or floor can we be sure that the carpet was on the floor.

The first hooked or pulled rugs were most likely used off the floor. The art of rug hooking is, according to the authority William Winthrop Kent, a north-country invention. Scandinavians, Scots, and Dutch people introduced it to America. Perhaps the Pilgrims and Puritans got the idea from the Dutch.

Just when hooked rugs were made generally for floor use we cannot say for sure. It would seem, however, that the mid-eighteenth century marked the beginning of floor-rug production by this technique—a method that is essentially a home craft.

The earliest homemade rugs were not hooked. They were little more than an overlapping of pieces of cloth sewed upon a coarse homespun background, usually linen. This served the purpose but could scarcely be called artistic. With the aid of a dye pot, narrow strips of cloth, a piece of homespun linen or sacking, a rug hook, and a little imagination, the first hooked rug was evolved.

The linen backing was securely fastened to a frame not unlike a small quilting frame. Upon this stretched fabric the pattern was drawn. Narrow strips of material were pulled with a small hook through the coarse mesh of the foundation in loops following the design. Sometimes the loops were cut but frequently they were left just as they were hooked through. As in most primitive art, designs were suggested by everyday things. Garden flowers and animals were great favorites. In seaport towns it is quite natural that we should find ships and nautical devices executed with truly wonderful results. The "Welcome" rugs carry a good old feeling of hospitality and friendliness. Geometric designs were sometimes used, though it is difficult to find a rug that has regular outline. The coarsely woven fabric of the background was not the best thing upon which to draw a straight line or circle. In random flower patterns such irregularities pass unnoticed.

The hooked rug is one "antique" that owes much to one Pond, of Biddeford, Maine, who, in 1877, began the manufacture of hooked-rug patterns. These patterns were stenciled on burlap and were sold, by an extensive advertising campaign, in every state in the Union. Maine housewives used Pond patterns by the thousand. They had the rags, the hooks, and the time on their hands. Carloads of hooked rugs—old rugs, as hooked rug ages go—came out of Maine in the 1920s. Carloads still come

WHEEL of FORTUNE

NORTH CAROLINA LILY

JACOB'S LADDER

CONVENTIONAL TULIP

SUNBURST

LOG CABIN

CHARTER OAK

ROSE WREATH

ROSE of SHARON

PRINCESS FEATHERS

me of the most popular quilt patterns of the last half of the eighteenth century and the first half of the nineteenth century are here pictured.

from Maine and from New Brunswick. Pond did not originate the commercialization of hooked-rug patterns. Edward Frost has that distinction. Frost was an invalid soldier of the Civil War who turned to peddling and who, lacking a stock to peddle, conceived the idea of stenciling hooked-rug patterns in 1870.

Most of the hooked rugs today coming out of New England and other states are of modern make, if not modern design. They are sometimes the result of home industry and sometimes of shop production. Most of them are made in winter for summer sale to dealers and tourists. Some of these rugs in late Victorian genre designs have brought fantastic prices at auctions. It takes no longer to hook a jovial and nostalgic genre scene on a rug than to hook an old conventional pattern. But when the genre rugs sell as high as three hundred dollars and the conventional sells at thirty dollars, who wouldn't hook the genre rug?

Braided rugs may not appeal so much to one's nostalgic imagination as the hooked rug, but some very charming examples have been found. In making these rugs the material was cut in narrow strips and plaited in flat braids. The braids were then sewed together along the edges, making an oval or circular rug. When well made, these rugs lie flat on the floor and retain their shape indefinitely. Sometimes several rows of braiding were put around a hooked rug for a finishing touch. For the lover of antiques there is almost always something fascinating about an old rug, no matter what the color or design.

One of the strictly feminine crafts coming down to us from colonial days is quilt making. Many of the early methods, as well as patterns, are still in use today in the remote mountain sections of North Carolina. All the hardships of pioneer days could not suppress the love of the beautiful, and the creative, homemaking genius of woman found its self-expression in working out the intricate designs of these bedcoverings.

Until the nineteenth century the bed held an important and conspicuous position as an article of furnishing. Houses had few rooms and we often find a bed in a hallway or living room. Naturally the housewife took great pride in its equipment and spent many hours on the hangings and coverings. It is to be supposed that the colonists brought some bedcoverings from England though this supply must have been limited and soon standing in need of replenishment. As bedcovers were also used to hang over doors and windows to keep out the wintry drafts, we can see that many of them were needed even in a comparatively small home.

On the large Southern plantations and in the great manor houses of the North, where entertaining was lavish, slaves and hired help were taught to weave. Quilts, whether patched, pieced, or woven, were made in all of the colonies, and the fact that similar and even identical designs were found all over the country leads us to suppose that some of the patterns used were old and were brought from England, Holland, or France.

Woven coverlets were given various colloquial names in different sections. They were made on a hand loom thirty inches wide in two strips of the desired length and then sewed together to make a spread. The warp was usually of white cotton or linen—sometimes of candlewicking—and the woof of colored wool. In many cases these materials were grown, spun into thread or yarn, dyed, and woven into coverlets by the housewife. Later there were professional itinerant weavers who, traveling from house to house, used the yarn that had been made ready for them on the looms of their patrons. Others had looms set up in their places of business. Being more broadly experienced, they were able to weave more intricate patterns more speedily. Some looms were made wide enough to weave an entire spread in one piece. These coverlets are much in demand today.

The women of colonial times were most skillful in the making of vegetable dyes which have retained their luster and brilliancy throughout the years. Blue and red were favorites, but yellow, pink, green, and brown were used. Black runs through many of the designs. It was always necessary to use a mordant to set the dye, and slum and sometimes copperas served this purpose. Indigo made any shade of blue, depending upon how long the material was left in the dye. If the wool had been sun-burned it turned blue-green when dipped into indigo. All reds from rose to claret could be obtained with cochineal, and when diluted the pinks resulted. The barks of the walnut, chestnut, and hickory gave a brown dye, and black oak and hickory made green. For a lovely light green the shell of the young butternut was best. Sumac, saffron, goldenrod, wild cherry, laurel and peach leaves gave various yellows, and scrub oak, log wood, or nut galls, black. This is by no means a complete list of dyes but will serve to give an idea of the variety of materials from which dyes could be made.

In the pieced and sewn quilt we find such a variety of colors and designs that a classification is almost useless. The earliest covers were made for durability and are not so artistic as those produced when the housewife had more time to devote to their making and designing. Cotton and linen were favorite materials, no doubt because they were easily obtainable. Silk, satin, and velvet cloths appear but were never used to any great extent.

Simplest of all the designs was the plain pieced work cover made of small blocks five or six inches square. Each of these blocks was in turn made of smaller pieces in two or more colors. It is readily seen how practical

HOOKED RUGS

these covers were, for the minutest scraps of material could be used in them. Some blocks were units in themselves although often a part of a large pattern, usually geometric in design. The "star" patterns are always lovely. These are made of small triangular pieces forming a star and so arranged in color that the whole design shades from the center of the star to the edge.

Appliquéd quilts required more skill than those that were pieced because the design was cut out and sewed down upon a solid background of another piece of material. These motifs could be made of a solid color or of blending or contrasting colors. The background was generally white linen or unbleached muslin. For convenience they were also worked in small blocks and sewn together when the required number was finished. In addition to the top and back a third thickness of material, an interlining, was added and held to the front or back with fine hand stitching called quilting, done on a frame made for the purpose. The quilting frame consisted of four narrow pieces of wood with holes in either end of each. Two of the pieces were longer than the quilt and two shorter. Some of these frames stood on uprights above the height of a table, but the majority of them were pegged at the corners to form a rectangle and placed on the backs of four chairs for support. The edges of the frame were bound with strips of cloth and to these the quilt was basted to hold it firmly. As one end of the quilting was finished the rod was detached and rolled back.

Over the lining was spread a thin layer of wool or cotton and then the pieced top. Great care was taken to keep the edges of the quilt even and the pattern was then drawn. This consisted of single, double, or triple lines running diagonally across the whole in squares, diamonds, shells, pineapples, fans, and ostrich-feather designs. They were all outlined in a fine running stitch, sometimes as many as twenty stitches to the inch. It took a tremendous amount of patience and time to produce some of the marvelous quilting found in the old coverlets. Elaborate centers and corners against a background so closely quilted that it threw the pattern in relief were not uncommon. Sometimes the design was raised by stuffing it with cotton forced through the open mesh of the lining, with a sharp-pointed instrument resembling a needle, after the quilt was removed from the frame. We find many names of varied suggestion attached to the quilts of this time: "The Lincoln Platform," "The Democratic Rose," and the "Prince of Wales Feathers" are a few famous ones.

The most beautiful of all American quilts were produced in the late eighteenth century.

In the old wills of our earliest history we find damask and turkeywork mentioned so frequently that we may suppose them to have been popular materials. The damask was costly even then, and usually imported from England or France. Turkeywork is merely another name for worsted work—generally upon canvas in cross-stitch. The name seems to have come from the fact that turkeywork first appears in imitation of small Turkish rugs used as covers on tables. Turkeywork is hooked rug making in miniature. A large needle is used to draw wool through the mesh.

The earliest known mention of samplers in England is in 1502, yet somehow we find it difficult to dissociate the sampler from colonial America. The lettered legends on these bits of fabric hold for us so personal an element of social history that it is difficult to associate them with any other period or place.

The earliest samplers in this country were long and narrow. The upper portion was filled with elaborate

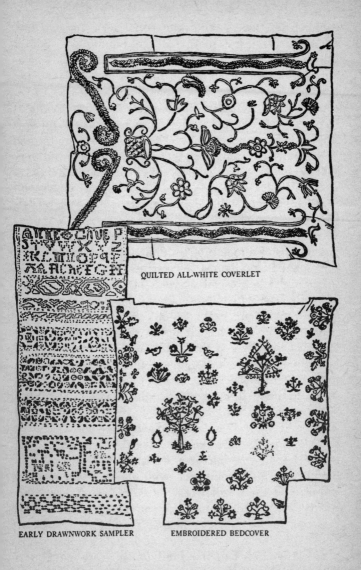

QUILTED ALL-WHITE COVERLET

EARLY DRAWNWORK SAMPLER   EMBROIDERED BEDCOVER

running designs. In the center appeared a "tree of life" or other allegorical motif. At the bottom was cut or drawn work with an occasional alphabet worked in as an integral part of the design. Only two of the authentic examples of seventeenth-century samplers exist. Eighteenth-century samplers were made in large numbers throughout the colonies, but more particularly in New England, Long Island, New Jersey, and Pennsylvania. The first were English in type but were followed very shortly by the development of a distinctly American style.

Stitching and embroidery were taught in all schools for girls. One class of sampler comes from this source. The other class is composed of samplers made by very young girls as a means of learning not only stitching but the alphabet and figures. Such samplers were often made by girls of but five and six years of age and, while simple compared with those made in the boarding-schools, are still marvelous examples of patience and skill.

About 1721 American samplers began to display biblical scenes. A few of these are known with the legends in Latin. Alphabets were separated from the patterns by rows of cross-stitch, Greek fret, or equally simple designs. Running designs display the "India pink," tulip with vines, and the "tree of life." Pennsylvania at this time contributed samplers displaying the Lord's Prayer and the Ten Commandments. Many fine samplers were almost needlework pictures, so large and prominent is the picture part compared with the borders, and so exquisite is the needlework. In 1738 Boston came forward with an Adam and Eve sampler design, and for many years this subject remained popular.

By 1750 the heavy religious feeling in sampler work was lost and we find the motifs taken from nature and daily life. Of this period a beautiful Dorothy Linde

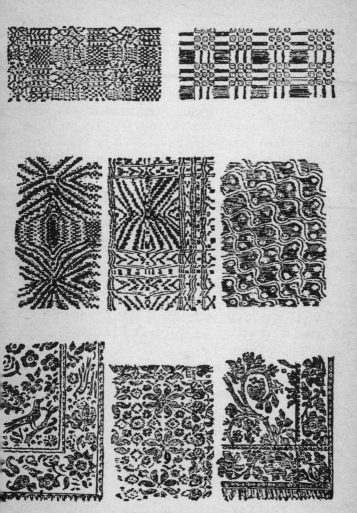

EIGHT EXAMPLES OF WOVEN COVERLETS

sampler remains in the Old South Church of Boston. Both coloring and lettering are unusual and the whole sampler is worked in petit point. Variants appear at every turn that cannot be placed in the categories mentioned above, but this does not exclude them from their places among worthy American samplers.

After 1760 the religious feeling is again apparent in most of the samplers that survive. We are able to trace these style movements with fair accuracy because many of the samplers are dated. Virginia made samplers of the 1760s that display the Adam and Eve motif. In this same decade, Boston samplers began to picture groups of buildings. One young lady, Bath-Sheba Searing, in 1766 pictured an entire village on her sampler. In 1755 Miss Frances Breton of Rhode Island executed a map of Newport on her sampler.

If one cared to do so—and this is a project worthy of consideration—it would be possible to identify the influence of many girls' schools in the samplers made by pupils. Another interesting bit of research would be the tracing of American sampler designs to their sources in old-world pattern books. A book of this type, titled *A Schole-House for the Needle*, dated London, 1632, was issued by a master named Shorleyker. In some copies this book is dedicated to Mistress Saltonstall, wife of the lord mayor. A bibliography of old-world pattern books by Arthur Lotz, published at Leipzig in 1933, discloses the fact that the Netherlands, Germany, France, Italy, Switzerland, and England enjoyed scores of design books printed not only for the women and girls but for the professional lace and fabric weavers, artists and decorators. Italy and Switzerland seem to have been the first to publish designs from the Near East.

Pennsylvania and New York samplers show many design elements which are pure Scandinavian, yet these same samplers, in Pennsylvania, show also some Swiss and English designs, while the samplers of New York State reflect early Dutch motifs. Naturally these designs jumped colonial borders and appeared in other places.

Early letters often mention homemade as well as imported lace on the wearing apparel of both men and women. Little is known of its early manufacture except a detailed account written up in an old history of Ipswich, Massachusetts, by one Felt. He describes the making of this lace upon pillows. The pattern, drawn upon parchment, was attached to the pillow and the entire design outlined with pins stuck upright into the cushion. About them was woven the design. The thread, usually linen, was wound upon bobbins made of chicken bone and uniquely, in America, of bamboo. By 1790 Felt estimates the yearly output of this industry at 41,979 yards. With the advent of machinery, the pillows and bobbins were discarded although the making of lace was still taught to children.

At Midway, Massachusetts, the Rev. Horace Dean Walker had a machine of 1,260 shuttles which attracted attention from far and wide. Net was manufactured here and sent with patterns into neighboring homes to be embroidered. Sometimes the designs were made by the embroiderer and are usually painstaking in detail.

Lacemaking was taught in the Moravian School at Bethlehem, Pennsylvania, and in Miss Pierce's Female Academy at Litchfield, Connecticut. Many of the girls educated in these schools carried their work to the point of making exquisite dresses and wedding veils.

It is impossible here to go into a lengthy outline of lacemaking, but after 1800 every current magazine picked up the fad. Darned laces upon net appeared in two popular designs, "the cat's eye" and "two and thripenny," from the Ipswich manufactory. Later came an embroidered and linen tape lace.

One thing should be evident to the casual reader on this excursion into needle and loom work. There is much yet to be done in research on the American phases of these ancient arts.

Chapter XXI

CLOCKS

THE small number of clocks surviving from our first colonial century is owing to several causes. First of all there were not many clocks owned per capita between 1620 and 1680. Next, most of those were imported, and the few which may have been made here in that period were either relegated to scrap piles with the coming of newer and better clocks or the metal parts were used in making other clocks. Some few of them, suffering neither of these modes of destruction, were so thoroughly modernized, revamped, and rebuilt as to become, in effect, new clocks. When this happened, and it did happen, the old clock was fitted with a pendulum and put in a new case. Of course we know what kinds of clocks our early settlers must have had—they had clocks from England, the Netherland, a few from France, and perhaps some from Sweden. Their clocks were quite similar to those used generally in the homelands of the settlers. We know our early colonists had clocks because there are documents that mention clocks. But we have only a very precious few of the clocks mentioned in those documents.

In the early days of the vogue for Americana and the collecting of antiques there was considerable importing of old English and Dutch clocks made in the seventeenth century. Within the past several decades expert appraisal has put certain of these imports under the microscope of close inspection and analysis. This study reveals that the imports which are not outright fakes are still questionable in terms of original condition. Most of them show signs of considerable repair and replacement. Generally speaking the clocks miscalled bracket clocks, made in the seventeenth century up to about 1680, are not bracket clocks at all. They require no "bracket" or shelf of any kind. They are spring-driven clocks which, when wound up, will run anywhere they are placed. Conversely, the clocks of this period commonly called "bird cage," "bedpost," and other names are real bracket clocks. They are weight-driven clocks requiring a firm position on the wall from which the weights could drop. Hence every one of them required a bracket or shelf. Some of the spring-driven clocks and most of the weight-driven clocks have short or "bob" pendulums. Those not equipped with pendulums have a form of balance wheel. After 1680 there was a tremendous flurry of business for clockmakers in converting all kinds of existing clocks into pendulum, or long-pendulum, timekeepers. The vogue for casing the clocks so modernized caused many repairmen to strip the older brass or wood casings from the clocks, saving only the dial and movement for inclusion in a new-fangled "tall case."

This is the type of clock we now call "grandfather," but which was never known by that name until a nineteenth-century writer wrote a poem about his grandfather's old clock. This also is the type of clock with which we must begin geographic consideration of colonial clock production. The details of movement construction, pendulum swing, and other mysteries of clock-making are not subjects for this volume. We must concern ourselves with clocks as antiques; with the complete unit made and sold as a device for telling time.

Colonial clockmaking may be said to have started by

1680. The places of making were Massachusetts, Connecticut, Delaware (or the Delaware section of Pennsylvania), Penn's ".Sylvania," and New York. By 1700 it is believed that there were also some clockmakers at work in Maryland and Carolina. We must be careful how we word every sentence of this text and hence will amend that last statement to explain its meaning. We should say that there were clockmakers at work who not only repaired existing clocks and modernized them, but who also made new clocks. Perhaps the greatest rarity in the field of American antiques is a clock made by a colonial clockmaker between 1680 and 1700. We know there were clocks made; we know there were clockmakers at work. But their production failed to survive the years save in numbers that makes any example almost unique.

During the first half of the eighteenth century clockmakers were at work in most colonial settlements of any importance. That most of them were at work in New England can be explained by the fact that in New England most of the villages and towns were located. The Pilgrim century of town planting simply dotted the New England landscape with populated places. By 1700 these towns had begun to grow. Today a study of the various states for cities and towns boasting populations ranging from ten thousand up to one hundred thousand reveals that Massachusetts is first by long odds. Many of these places were on the map in the first half of the eighteenth century. Clockmakers were at work in Charleston, Annapolis, Wilmington, Williamsburg, Philadelphia, Lancaster; in the towns of New Jersey, Yonkers and Albany, New York; in scores of towns in Connecticut, Rhode Island, and Massachusetts.

The clocks made in ever-increasing numbers by an ever-increasing number of clockmakers constitute the pool from which we draw most of our early—or very

CLOCK BY
WILLIAM CLAGGETT EARLY PINE CLOCK

CLAGGETT
GRANDFATHER CLOCK

early—clocks. In *American Clocks and Clockmakers* (Doubleday, 1947), by one of the authors of this present work, more than 3,000 American clockmakers are listed. By far the majority of these makers were working after 1750. Yet most of those listed as working up to 1800 were clockmakers who knew this to be a fact: no two clocks made up to that year were made precisely alike. Variations in case design and movement construction make every example unique, at least to those who know their clocks. That many of them seem to be alike as two peas in a pod is because we look for the similarities and not for the dissimilarities. Whether we know it or not, we are prone to examine clocks as objects within categories or types and not as individual objects. This isn't objectionable at all. Otherwise only experts can afford to collect. And to be an expert one must be endowed with considerably more than an infinite capacity for taking pains. One must be endowed with almost unlimited funds and be able to make collecting —or expertizing—a life work. Those who make a career of antiques study as museum officials are, luckily, able to enjoy such endowment of time and money. Most collectors have bread-and-butter tasks to perform and take their collecting as one of the pleasures of life. Therefore, the following classification of early American tall case clocks by categories, borrowed from *American Clocks and Clockmakers*, will satisfy the needs of the average, and even the above-average, collector:

1680–1700 Flat-topped cases of simple cabinetworks, some with paneled doors, some with hoods or heads having twist-turned and twist-carved pillars, and with "chests" or bottoms standing squarely on the floor. Paneled or plain doors. This style, generally, is "William and Mary."

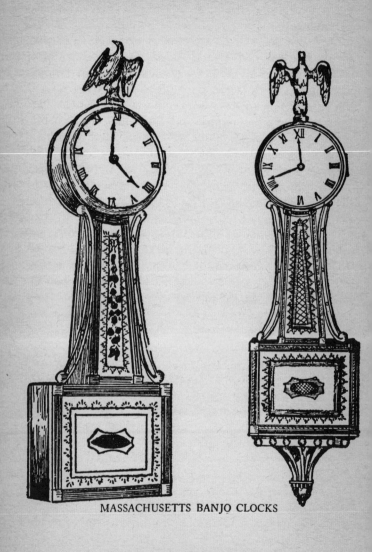

MASSACHUSETTS BANJO CLOCKS

1700–1710 Flat-topped cases capped with elevations in the form of shaped coffers or caskets called "bell-tops," twist-carved and turned pillars, with chests resting squarely on the floor or with bun feet. Paneled doors. Redolent of the William and Mary style.

1710–1725 Arched tops, conforming somewhat to the arch of the dial; rounded tops, generally finished off with a molding, light or heavy. Turned and carved side pillars on hoods. Bun or ball feet. A few with ogee feet. Paneled doors, some with arched tops, sometimes carved with a shell or sunburst. William and Mary converted to "Queen Anne" or early Georgian styling.

1725–1750 Arched and "broken-arch" tops, some embellished with fretwork similar to that found on tops of Queen Anne and early Georgian mirrors. Brass and turned-wood finials. Turned pillars on hoods. Ogee or "S"-curved feet. Paneled doors with carvings and sometimes with carving over the face of the hood section above the dials.

1750–1770 Scroll tops, fine carving on hood fronts, turned pillars, carved and molded finials, shell carvings, and block fronting on doors and many superior elements of Georgian and Chippendale styling. Cases made at Philadelphia, Newport, and in the suburban village of Lampeter, near Lancaster, Pennsylvania, in this period approximate the best that London and Paris cabinetmakers were producing. Bachman, the casemaker near Lancaster, was a Swiss-trained cabinetmaker working in the French style. He did not make cases in the form they were made in France. He followed the English or American tall-case styles but worked in the French tradition. Chippendale borrowed many of

BRACKET CLOCK BY ELI TERRY

his designs from the same source. The Georgian ball-and-claw foot, the ogee, and others, including the French foot, appear on these clocks.

After 1776 there was very little clockmaking until the Revolution ended. By 1782 a few clockmakers had returned to work. The war that had been won did more than give the colonists the liberty and freedom they had wanted. It put responsibilities for a new peacetime economy and a new social order squarely in the laps of all the people. Former clockmakers who had turned to war production were loath to return to clockmaking. A catalyst was needed all down the line, not only in clockmaking but in gunsmithing, furniture making, tinsmithing, pewtering, silversmithing, to resolve, in the minds of the artisans, the unrecognized "something" they had been shooting at, and for, in the Revolution. When they made the discovery they were amazed at the simplicity of it: increase production and you increase the earning capacity of all involved in production and at the same time can lower the price of the finished article. There was the key to the new American economy. There was the formula for the creation of hundreds and thousands of little mints where money was earned, not coined, and by which wealth was distributed and made common.

The first clockmakers to grasp this idea were the men of Connecticut. It is necessary to recite their story here. We have stated that Connecticut spells chests, chairs, and clocks. It does. What is important, however, is the story within the story of post-Revolutionary clockmaking in the new federation of states. While the clockmakers of Connecticut were making the experiments that led to mass production, all over the American scene clockmakers were experimenting with the idea of making more clocks, and a wider variety of clocks. After 1785 one of the most delightful clocks ever conceived was made by our native makers—a small size tall-case clock that could be placed on the floor, on a mantel, or on a shelf—the clock we call a "grandmother."

This type of clock was made in so many forms that today we don't even recognize them as sisters under the skin, or case. Basically the idea sprang from the desire for smaller clocks, for a clock that would go into a case half the size of a tall-case. The Willards, up in Massachusetts, made their smaller clocks in several forms, the most generally known being the "case-on-case" clock. The Willards also made an exceptionally fine smaller clock which, running under a bell of glass mounted on a decorative pedestal, now rejoices in the name of "lighthouse." Other clockmakers just cased their smaller clocks in smaller sized tall-cases. Still others cased them in variations of tall-cases which eventually became the designs for mantel clock cases. Simon Willard finally developed a remarkably accurate small clock that would run eight days with one winding. This he patented and offered for sale in the case we call the "banjo." The case shape was not a new idea. The Willard version was new in size and an immediate sensation. Other makers used the lyre-form case and variants of it which, as a case idea, came from France. Willard and other Massachusetts clockmakers turned to the hanging wall clock as their major answer to the public desire for smaller clocks.

Connecticut clockmakers turned to the shelf clock as their answer. The Connecticut clockmakers made millions of dollars out of their good guess that a mantel or shelf clock was what most of the people wanted. Meanwhile, between 1785 and 1840, thousands of clockmakers continued to produce grandfather clocks. By far the greater number of so-called grandfather clocks was

EARLY CLOCKS BY CONNECTICUT AND
MASSACHUSETTS MAKERS

made in this period. Which is to say that more than half of the grandfather clocks now extant are not colonial clocks at all—they are clocks made in our federal era.

These clocks, especially the ones made after 1800, display Sheraton, Hepplewhite, and Directoire style influences although some of them are as redolent of Queen Anne, the Georgian period, and Chippendale as cases made in those periods. Dials almost invariably are painted. The finer clocks have sweep second hands, moon-phase indicators, and other special features such as the day of the month indicated by a hand on the dial or through a slot in the dial. On the clocks of this period we find the motion or "clock-is-running" indicators in the form of rocking ships, rolling eyes in a face or several faces, nodding heads, fisherman casting rod, children on seesaw, and so on.

In spite of certain professional collecting trends and vogues for types of clocks, the best clocks are the eight-day, brass-movement time-and-strike examples, whether in tall cases, grandmother cases, wall cases, or mantel or shelf cases. Perhaps the most popular clock today is the Terry pillar-and-scroll cased wooden one-day movement invented by Eli Terry. Terry did not invent the pillar-and-scroll case; he invented the simple, all-wood movement by which this clock could be made cheaply and sold cased for the amazingly low sum of fifteen dollars. Because, to most people, a pillar-and-scroll isn't genuine unless it is a Terry, one of the finest pillar-and-scroll clocks ever offered for sale went begging for a buyer. This clock, an eight-day brass movement by Heman Clark of Plymouth, Connecticut, is in its original pillar-and-scroll casing, with the engraved label of the maker. It is a finer clock than any pillar-and-scroll by Terry and is, most likely, the clock he copied, as to

EMPIRE PILLAR CLOCK

BRACKET CLOCK SHOWING LATE EMPIRE
INFLUENCE

casing, in order to make his low-priced one-day wooden-movement mantel clock look rich and rare.

When we collect clocks and refuse to follow trends, we are apt to do much better for ourselves. But of course there are two schools of clock collectors. The one school, to which both the authors of this work subscribe, collects clocks to use in the home as part and parcel of the decorative scheme. We want these clocks to have good and original movements. But we want to wind the clocks as infrequently as possible. Hence we prefer the eight-day clocks. Most collectors of this school have an interest in the clocks of almost every era from 1700 to 1840 because their other antiques interests embrace objects made in these same years.

The other school of clock collectors are movement enthusiasts. They are as much concerned with variants of weight suspension, spring-type, pendulum swing and placement, wheel train arrangement, and other technical details as the first school is concerned with case style. The beauty lovers will stand off and admire the *tout ensemble* of clock-in-case. The movement enthusiasts cannot wait to open doors and remove hoods and dials in order to examine, and gloat, over the movement. Both types of collectors are quite sane about it. It's just a matter of where the interest resides. Because of this interest in movement construction we other collectors hear about unusual clocks that interest us not a little. For example, Joseph Ives, perhaps the greatest unpublicized genius in American clockmaking, invented a clock that ran by a wagon spring. He used the tremendous power that is in a leaf spring of the wagon type to run a clock a week, and even thirty days. In 1825 Ives began production of these "wagon-spring" clocks in Brooklyn. Tradition says he bought some cases from Duncan Phyfe. This may not be the fact, but tradition

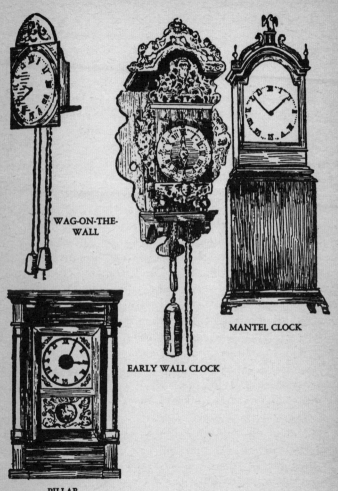

WAG-ON-THE-
WALL

EARLY WALL CLOCK

MANTEL CLOCK

PILLAR
BRACKET CLOCK

was justified in attributing the case to Phyfe because it is of a design comparable to Phyfe's furniture of that day. We confess to having a great desire for a thirty-day wagon-spring clock in such a case. Further confession must include this statement: it would be a relief to have an old clock we had to wind only twelve times a year. Winding clocks isn't the chore—it's remembering to wind them, in this age of electricity and automatic service, that is the task.

A Connecticut clock man, George Marsh of Farmington, emigrated to Ohio in 1831. In 1832 he formed a company for making clocks and by 1833 the firm of Marsh, Williams & Company was in business, "the first clock company in the West." This factory produced twenty-five hundred clocks a year.

In New York State, Asa Munger, at Auburn, had a small clock factory. He made a unique number now known as the "stovepipe" clock. The name is well applied. Two pieces of stovepipe (of small diameter) serve as columns on either side of the case. In these columns are hidden the weights that drive the clock.

The Timby solar clock was made in New York State. This clock, highly touted by certain clock enthusiasts, was made as a novelty for sale to the tourists at Saratoga. A small globe of the earth is poised within a shallow casing, projecting back and front. The clock designates the time on each meridian by bringing the meridians under an indicator. This clock was made about 1850 to 1860.

Innumerable novelty clocks were made by scores of makers who, in the hurly-burly of competition, were attempting and trying various types of novelty clocks in the hope of making a killing. Chauncey Jerome's "bronzed looking-glass clock" was such a novelty. It wasn't a bronzed looking glass in a clock case. It was a cheap clock with one column split to provide stick-on columns for either side, painted with bronze and fitted with a looking-glass panel in the door instead of the more expensive hand-painted panel. This clock became so popular that a church in Bristol, Connecticut, was built on the bounty of those who profited by its making. It was called the "Bronzed Looking-Glass Clock Church." That Jerome appropriated the idea for this clock from Joseph Ives is perhaps no longer important. That he likewise borrowed, without so much as a thank you, his idea for his low-priced all-brass-movement clock from the same man *is* important. Jerome, in taking Ives's idea for a cheap brass clock, made that clock in such numbers that he revolutionized the clock industry of Connecticut and made a new industry, brass rolling, come to life.

As antiques collectors we may not be concerned with the birth of the rolled-brass industry of Connecticut, but we are concerned with what the brass clock did in terms of creating what are today considered antique clocks. It caused the making of millions of clocks in a variety of case designs beyond the capacity of one book, let alone a chapter, even to list and describe them! Yes, most of these clocks were made after 1840. But amazingly, these clocks are those most generally bought and sold as antiques. Even the cheap $2.50 one-day, brass cottage clocks of 1875 are now in antiques shops bearing price tags reading $25.

Clocks were made in all of the colonies and in the original thirteen states, plus Ohio. Nothing more need be said except this: until mass production was started, or sparked, by Eli Terry, first with hang-up clocks, uncased, and then with his pillar-and-scroll, most of the clocks were one of a kind.

After 1815 we find uniformity of production in clocks

of a type, but an almost immediate effort to make the "lines" or types of clocks as wide as possible. The result is a mass of clocks: the aristocracy being the clocks of real age and stateliness made up to 1770, the middle class the grandfather clocks made from 1771 to 1840, and the commonalty the mass-produced clocks of Connecticut. In this society are the banjo and lyre clocks of Massachusetts, the other masterpieces by Willard, and the occasional mantel clock made in the eighteenth century. Social lines are not sharply drawn. Common clocks and aristocratic clocks are to be found in many collectors' homes and in many famed clock collections. As in America itself, the common clocks sometimes reach fame and sometimes the aristocrats fall. But collecting clocks is still an Alice-in-Wonderland sort of adventure. The simile doesn't end there. The clock story, as well as Alice, is the result of mathematical thinking.

THE END

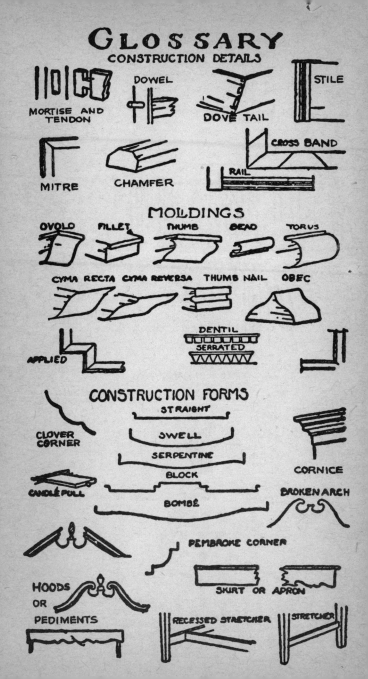

GLOSSARY
CONSTRUCTION DETAILS

MORTISE AND TENDON

DOWEL

DOVE TAIL

STILE

MITRE

CHAMFER

CROSS BAND

RAIL

MOLDINGS

OVOLO

FILLET

THUMB

BEAD

TORUS

CYMA RECTA

CYMA REVERSA

THUMB NAIL

OBEC

APPLIED

DENTIL
SERRATED

CONSTRUCTION FORMS

CLOVER CORNER

STRAIGHT

SWELL

SERPENTINE

BLOCK

BOMBÉ

CORNICE

CANDLE PULL

BROKEN ARCH

PEMBROKE CORNER

HOODS OR PEDIMENTS

SKIRT OR APRON

RECESSED STRETCHER

STRETCHER

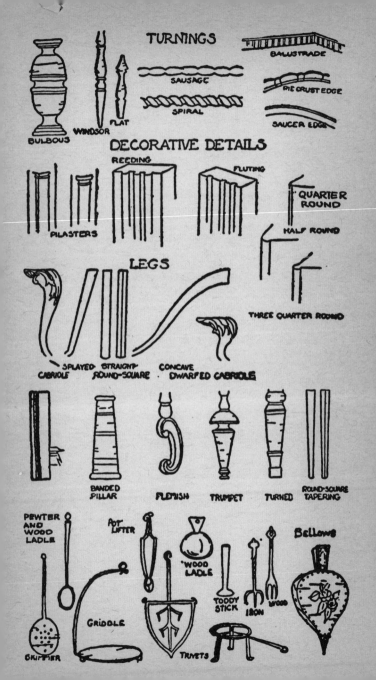

TURNINGS

BULBOUS
WINDSOR
FLAT
SAUSAGE
SPIRAL
BALUSTRADE
PIE CRUST EDGE
SAUCER EDGE

DECORATIVE DETAILS

REEDING
FLUTING
QUARTER ROUND
PILASTERS
HALF ROUND
THREE QUARTER ROUND

LEGS

CABRIOLE
SPLAYED
STRAIGHT ROUND-SQUARE
CONCAVE
DWARFED CABRIOLE

BANDED PILLAR
FLEMISH
TRUMPET
TURNED
ROUND-SQUARE TAPERING

PEWTER AND WOOD LADLE
POT LIFTER
WOOD LADLE
TODDY STICK
IRON
WOOD
Bellows

SKIMMER
GRIDDLE
TRIVETS

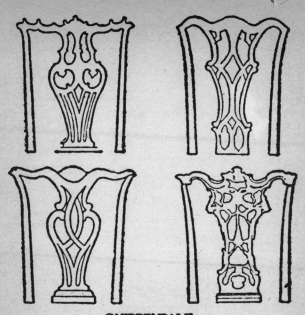

CHIPPENDALE
CHARACTERISTIC CHAIR BACKS
AND LEGS

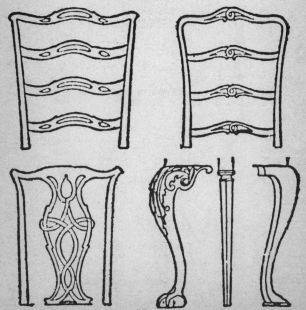

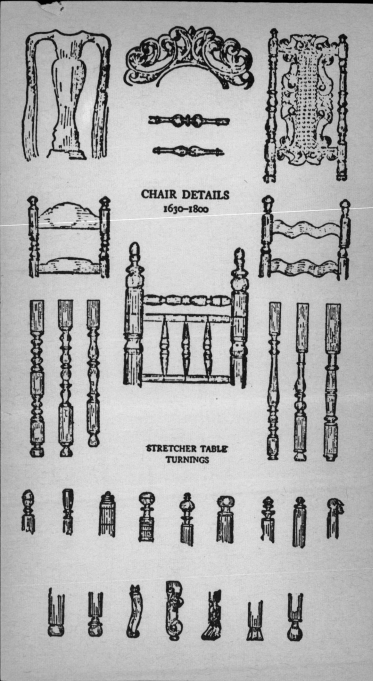

CHAIR DETAILS
1630–1800

**STRETCHER TABLE
TURNINGS**

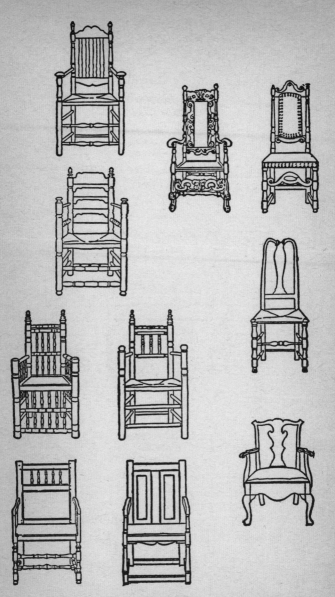

Chairs and sofas. The chairs, from lower left upward across top and down to lower right, constitute a parade as follows: the first two are wainscot type, second two are Carver and Brewster, next slat back, next banister back, next two are Flemish and

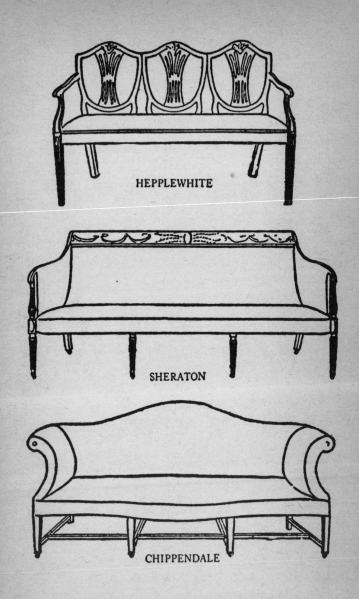

HEPPLEWHITE

SHERATON

CHIPPENDALE

Dutch chairs of William and Mary period, next an early Queen Anne cottage-type, and next Queen Anne-Georgian master chair. Pictured also are typical sofas of the periods indicated.

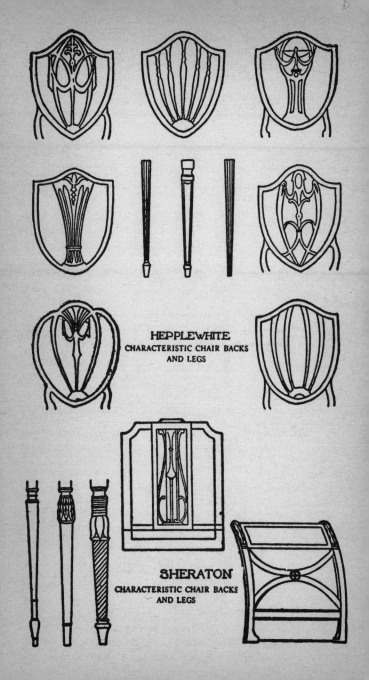

HEPPLEWHITE
CHARACTERISTIC CHAIR BACKS
AND LEGS

SHERATON
CHARACTERISTIC CHAIR BACKS
AND LEGS

BRASSES
1640–1800

TRIPOD STAND
WITH
KETTLE

WOODEN
MUG

FIRE-CARRIER

SKILLET

TINDER BOX

KETTLE

SPICE BOX

BIRD
TRAMMEL

FOOT-WARMER

TABLES

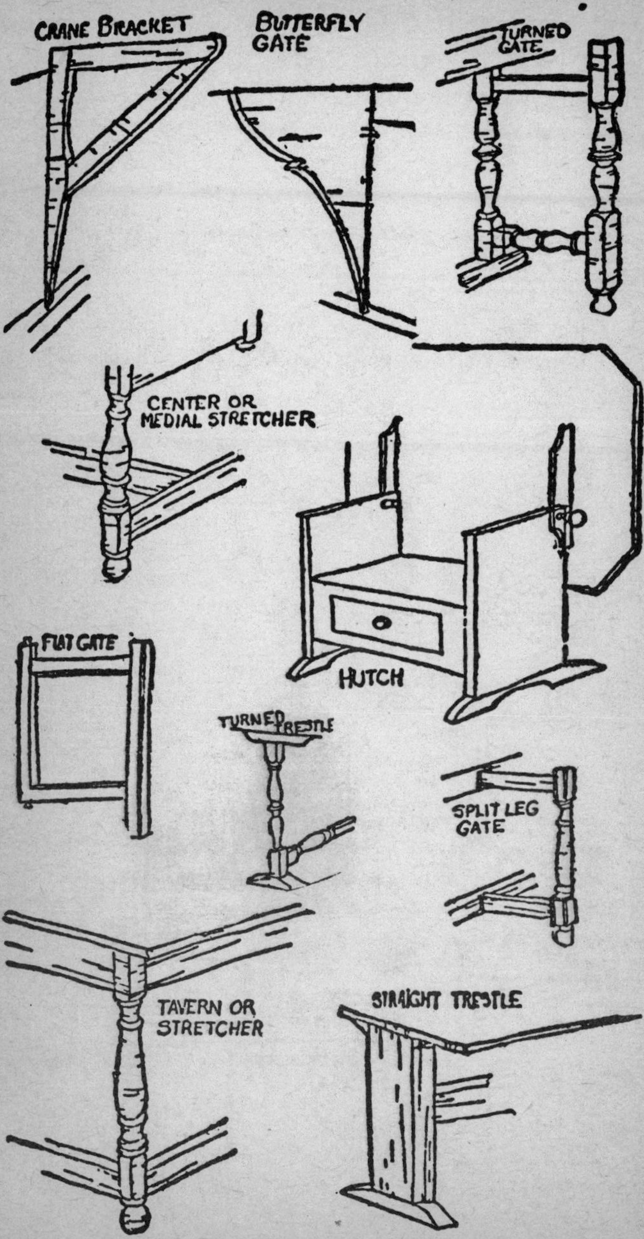

CRANE BRACKET

BUTTERFLY GATE

TURNED GATE

CENTER OR MEDIAL STRETCHER

FLAT GATE

TURNED TRESTLE

HUTCH

SPLIT LEG GATE

TAVERN OR STRETCHER

STRAIGHT TRESTLE

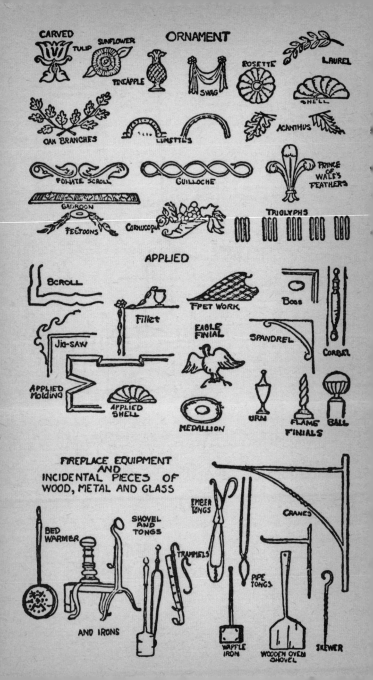

ORNAMENT

CARVED
TULIP
SUNFLOWER
PINEAPPLE
SWAG
ROSETTE
LAUREL
SHELL
OAK BRANCHES
LUNETTES
ACANTHUS
FOLIATE SCROLL
GUILLOCHE
PRINCE OF WALES FEATHERS
GADROON
FESTOONS
CORNUCOPIA
TRIGLYPHS

APPLIED

SCROLL
FILLET
FRET WORK
BOSS
JIG-SAW
EAGLE FINIAL
SPANDREL
CORBEL
APPLIED MOLDING
APPLIED SHELL
MEDALLION
URN
FLAME
BALL
FINIALS

FIREPLACE EQUIPMENT AND INCIDENTAL PIECES OF WOOD, METAL AND GLASS

BED WARMER
SHOVEL AND TONGS
EMBER TONGS
CRANES
AND IRONS
TRAMMELS
PIPE TONGS
WAFFLE IRON
WOODEN OVEN SHOVEL
SKEWER

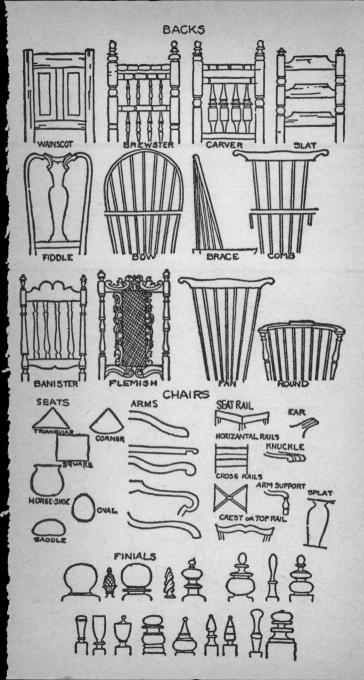

BACKS

WAINSCOT BREWSTER CARVER SLAT

FIDDLE BOW BRACE COMB

BANISTER FLEMISH FAN ROUND

CHAIRS

SEATS
TRIANGULAR CORNER SQUARE HORSE-SHOE OVAL SADDLE

ARMS

SEAT RAIL EAR
HORIZANTAL RAILS KNUCKLE
CROSS RAILS ARM SUPPORT SPLAT
CREST or TOP RAIL

FINIALS

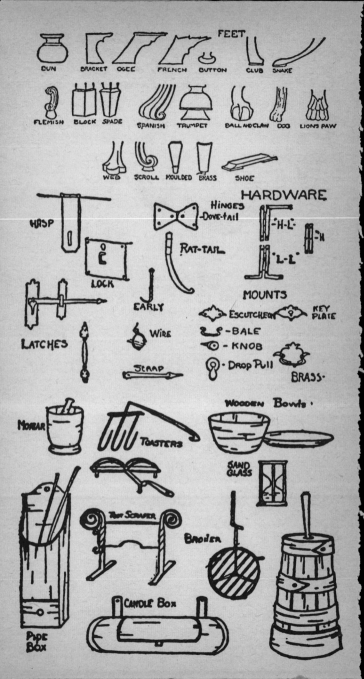

FEET

GUN · BRACKET · OGEE · FRENCH · BUTTON · CLUB · SNAKE

FLEMISH · BLOCK · SPADE · SPANISH · TRUMPET · BALL AND CLAW · DOG · LIONS PAW

WEB · SCROLL · MOULDED · BRASS · SHOE

HARDWARE

HASP

Hinges
-Dove-tail

"H-L"
"H"
"L-L"

RAT-TAIL

LOCK

MOUNTS

EARLY

Escutcheon · KEY PLATE

LATCHES

WIRE

·BALE

· KNOB

· Drop Pull

SCRAP

BRASS·

WOODEN BOWLS·

MORTAR

TOASTERS

SAND GLASS

TOE SCRAPER

BROILER

CANDLE BOX

PIPE BOX